Cambridge Primary

GW00391265

Hodder Cambridge Primary

Maths

Learner's Book

Stage 2

Catherine Casey

Series editors: Mike Askew
and Paul Broadbent

HODDER
EDUCATION
AN HACHETTE UK COMPANY

Author acknowledgements

With warm thanks to Jan Fisher for her help in shaping and developing this title.

The Publisher is extremely grateful to the following schools for their comments and feedback during the development of this series:
Avalon Heights World Private School, Ajman
The Oxford School, Dubai
Al Amana Private School, Sharjah
British International School, Ajman
Wesgreen International School, Sharjah
As Seeb International School, Al Khoud.
Practice test exam-style questions and sample answers are written by the author.

Photograph acknowledgements

We would like to thank the following for their permission to reproduce photographs:

p.7, p.5 © Fedotishe/123rf; **p.21, p.27 (both), p.68 (both), p.104 (all)** © Hachette UK; **p.23** © Pretoperola/123rf; **p.89** © Ocskay Bence Mor/123rf; **p.101** tl , **p.174** © Trodler/123rf; **p.101** tc © Ivan Fedorov/123rf; p.101 tr © Alan Waterman/Alamy Stock Photo; **p.101** bl © Wathanyu sowong /123rf; **p.101** bc © Февгений Косцов/123rf; **p.101** br © Zoonar GmbH/Alamy Stock Photo.

t = top, b = bottom, l = left, r = right, c = centre

Every effort has been made to trace all copyright holders, but if any have been inadvertently overlooked the Publishers will be pleased to make the necessary arrangements at the first opportunity.

Although every effort has been made to ensure that website addresses are correct at time of going to press, Hodder Education cannot be held responsible for the content of any website mentioned in this book. It is sometimes possible to find a relocated web page by typing in the address of the home page for a website in the URL window of your browser.

Hachette UK's policy is to use papers that are natural, renewable and recyclable products and made from wood grown in sustainable forests. The logging and manufacturing processes are expected to conform to the environmental regulations of the country of origin.

Orders: please contact Bookpoint Ltd, 130 Milton Park, Abingdon, Oxon OX14 4SB. Telephone: (44) 01235 827720. Fax: (44) 01235 400454. Lines are open from 9.00–5.00, Monday to Saturday, with a 24-hour message answering service. You can also order through our website www.hoddereducation.com

© Catherine Casey 2017

Published by Hodder Education

An Hachette UK Company

Carmelite House, 50 Victoria Embankment, London EC4Y 0DZ

Impression number   5

Year   2021 2020 2019

Cover illustrationby Steve Evans

Illustrations by Jeanne du Plessis and DTP Impressions

Typeset in FS Albert 17/19 by DTP Impressions

Printed in India

A catalogue record for this title is available from the British Library

9781471884337

Contents

Term 1

Term 2

I am Zara.

I am Ace.

Introduction

Explore the picture or problem.

What do you see? What can you find out?

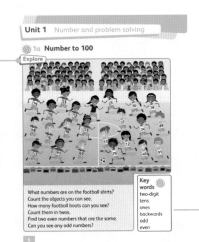

Key words are in a list for you to learn.

Learn new maths skills with your teacher.
Look at the diagrams to help you.

Practise the maths you have learnt. Write any answers in your exercise book.

Read these hints and tips to help you **think like a mathematician**.

Try this challenge activity to make you think carefully about the maths.

At the end of each unit try the **self-check** activities. What have you learnt?

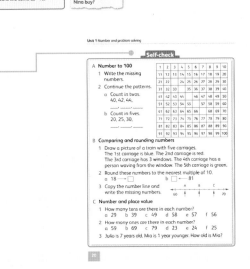

Unit 1   Number and problem solving

1a Number to 100

Explore

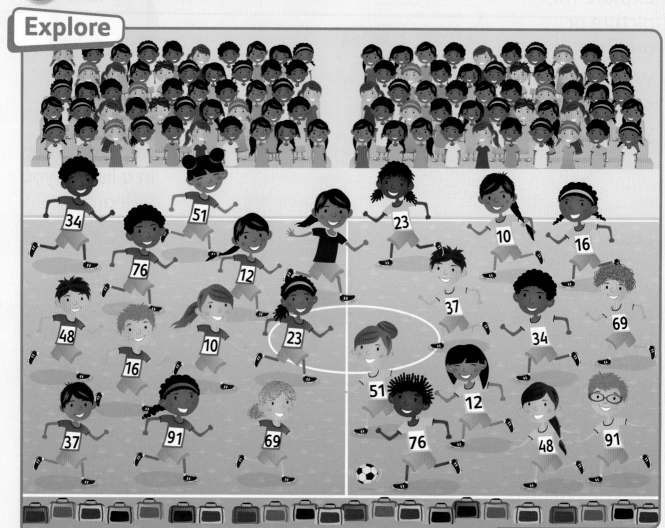

What numbers are on the football shirts?

Count the objects you can see.

How many football boots can you see?

Count them in twos.

Find two even numbers that are the same.

Can you see any odd numbers?

Key words
two-digit
tens
ones
backwards
odd
even

Count on and back in ones and tens

Learn

Count forwards from 30 to 40. What numbers are missing from the number track?

(30)(31)( )33 34 35( )37(38)(39)(40)

The numbers 32 and 36 are missing.

Count backwards from 40 to 30. What numbers are missing from the number track?

(40)(39)(38)( )36 35 34( )32(31)(30)

The numbers 33 and 37 are missing.

10, 9, 8, 7, 6, 5, 4, 3, 2, 1. Lift off!

Practise

1 Write the missing numbers. Work along each row.

a

| 41 | | 43 | 44 | 45 | | 47 | 48 | 49 |

b

| 51 | 52 | | 54 | | 56 | | 58 | 59 |

c

| 100 | | 80 | 70 | | 50 | 40 | 30 | 20 | | 0 |

2 Choose any two-digit number. Write down the next three numbers. Repeat.

For example: **34**, 35, 36, 37

Think like a mathematician

Look at a 100 square.
See how many patterns you can spot.

Try this

How many penguins can you see?

Count in twos, fives and tens

Learn

How many counters are there?

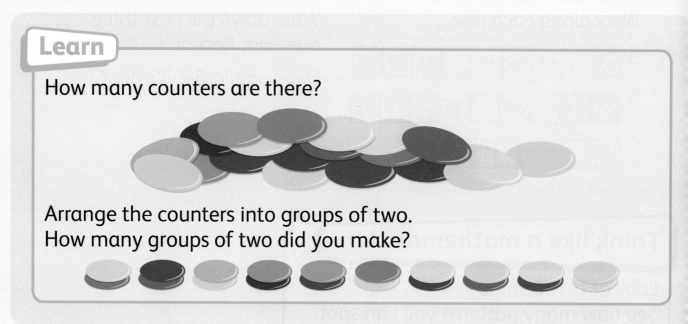

Arrange the counters into groups of two.
How many groups of two did you make?

Count in twos.
There are 20 counters.
These are all the even numbers up to 20.

2, 4, 6, 8, 10, 12, 14, 16, 18, 20

Show this on a number line.

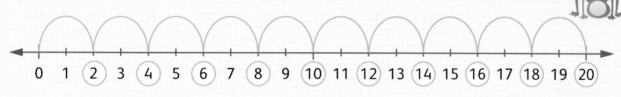

0 1 ② 3 ④ 5 ⑥ 7 ⑧ 9 ⑩ 11 ⑫ 13 ⑭ 15 ⑯ 17 ⑱ 19 ⑳

Which are the odd numbers?

Practise

1 Show how the frog jumps. Move your finger along the line.
   Write the numbers the frog lands on after each jump.
   The first one has been started for you.

   a Count in twos from 20 to 30.

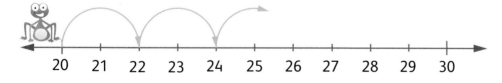

   b Count in fives from 30 to 60.

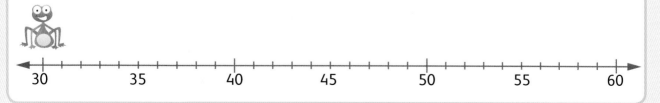

c Count in tens from 0 to 50.

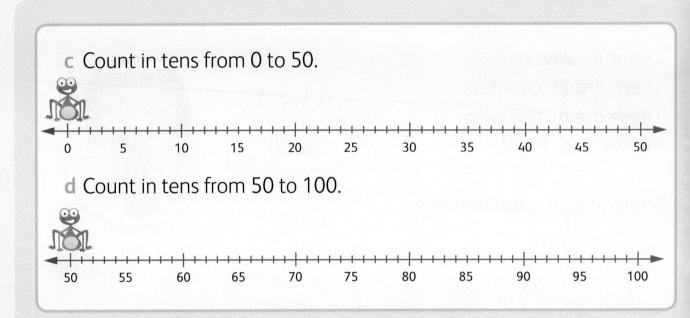

d Count in tens from 50 to 100.

Try this

A bee has 5 eyes. How many eyes do these bees have altogether?

There are 8 bees. How many eyes are there altogether?

There are 7 bees. How many eyes are there altogether?

There are 6 bees. How many eyes are there altogether?

There are 5 bees. How many eyes are there altogether?

1b Comparing and rounding numbers

Explore

In what order do the learners finish the race?

Look at the learners' positions and running times on the board. Some of the numbers are missing. Sara came second. Write all her possible times. Julio came fifth. Write all his possible times.

Key words

compare
order
ordinal
rounding
multiple
number line

RUNNING TIMES

1st : 60 seconds
2nd : ... seconds
3rd : 65 seconds
4th : 68 seconds
5th : ... seconds
6th : 72 seconds
7th : 76 seconds
8th : 81 seconds

Missing numbers

Learn

Which number is the arrow pointing to?

Count along the number line to the arrow. Point to each mark as you say the number.
The arrow is pointing to 24.

Practise

1 Write the numbers the arrows are pointing to.

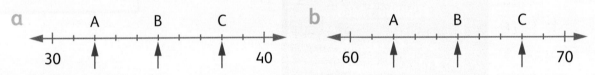

Rounding numbers

Learn

Some multiples of 10 are: 10, 20, 30, 40, 50, 60, 70, 80, 90, 100
We can round numbers up or down to the nearest multiple of 10.
Round **down** if the number is less than halfway. Round **up** if the number is halfway or more.

For example: 32 rounds down to 30
36 rounds up to 40.

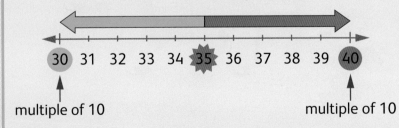

35 is halfway between 30 and 40.
35 rounds up to 40.

Practise

Round the numbers to the nearest 10. Use the number track.
The first one has been done for you.

| 10 | 20 | 30 | 40 | 50 | 60 | 70 | 80 | 90 | 100 |

20 ← 23   57 → ☐   ☐ ← 73

☐ ← 41   98 → ☐   66 → ☐

☐ ← 82   25 → ☐   ☐ ← 54

☐ ← 94   36 → ☐   87 → ☐

Think like a mathematician

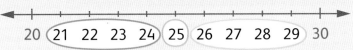

Look at the numbers in the loops. Which multiple of 10 is each number closest to? Are any numbers in the middle?

Ordering objects

Learn

Which carriage is orange? The 2nd carriage is orange.

Which carriage is blue? The 5th carriage is blue.

Which carriage is black? The 8th carriage is black.

2nd, 5th and 8th are ordinal numbers. We use them to order objects.

Practise

1 In what order did the cars finish? The first one has been done for you.

a The red car was 1st.

b The blue car was _____.

c The green car was _____.

d The yellow car was _____.

e The purple car was _____.

2 In what order did Lucia buy the fruit?

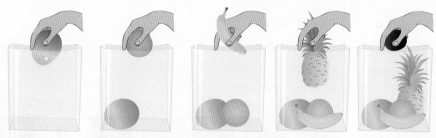

Lucia bought the:

a  _____.

b  _____.

c _____.

d  _____.

e  _____.

3 In what order are the children standing?

is _____ .   is _____ .   is _____ .   is _____ .   is _____ .

1c **Number and place value**

Explore

1	2	3	4	5	6	7	8	9	10
11	12	13	14	15	16	17	18	19	20
21	22	23	24	25	26	27	28	29	30
31	32	33	34	35	36	37	38	39	40
41	42	43	44	45	46	47	48	49	50
51	52	53	54	55	56	57	58	59	60
61	62	63	64	65	66	67	68	69	70
71	72	73	74	75	76	77	78	79	80
81	82	83	84	85	86	87	88	89	90
91	92	93	94	95	96	97	98	99	100

Key words
digit
tens
ones
more
less

I think of a number. I add 10. The answer is 29. What was my number?

Choose a number.

Write 1 more than that number.

Write 1 less than that number.

Write 10 more than that number.

Write 10 less than that number.

Use a hundred square. Colour the even numbers red. Colour the odd numbers green.

Tens and ones in two-digit numbers

What number does
the picture show?

How many tens?
How many ones?

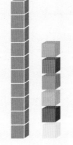

There is 1 ten: 10

There are 6 ones: 6

$10 + 6 = 16$

This shows the two-digit
number 16.

Tens	Ones
1	6

What number does
the picture show?

How many tens?
How many ones?

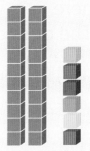

There are 2 tens: $10 + 10 = 20$

There are 6 ones: 6

$20 + 6 = 26$

This shows the two-digit
number 26.

Tens	Ones
2	6

1 Write the number to
match the picture.
The first one has been
done for you.

a Two tens and six ones
$20 + 6 = 26$

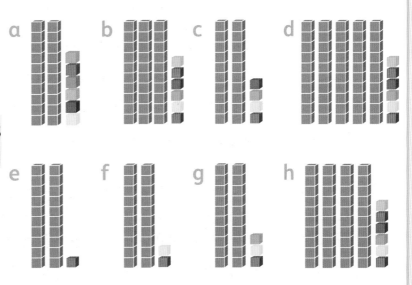

Try this

Elena has made a two-digit number. The tens are shown here.
The ones are hiding under the cup.
What could the number be?

Finding 1 more, 1 less, 10 more and 10 less

Learn

To make 1 more or 1 less, look at the ones.

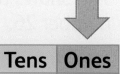

To make 10 more or 10 less, look at the tens.

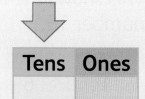

To make 1 **less**, take away 1.

1 less than 46 is 45.

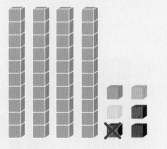

To make 10 **less**, take away 10.

10 less than 46 is 36.

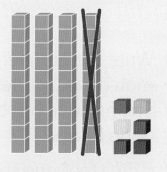

To make 1 **more**, add 1.

1 more than 46 is 47.

To make 10 **more**, add 10.

10 more than 46 is 56.

Practise

Do these calculations. You can use a 100 square to help you.
The first ones have been done for you.

1 34 + 1 = 35
35 + 1 = ☐
36 + 1 = ☐

88 + 1 = ☐
78 + 1 = ☐
68 + 1 = ☐

19 + 1 = ☐
29 + 1 = ☐
39 + 1 = ☐

2 79 − 1 = 78
78 − 1 = ☐
77 − 1 = ☐

42 − 1 = ☐
32 − 1 = ☐
22 − 1 = ☐

49 + 1 = ☐
59 + 1 = ☐
69 + 1 = ☐

3 51 + 10 = 61
52 + 10 = ☐
53 + 10 = ☐

64 + 10 = ☐
74 + 10 = ☐
84 + 10 = ☐

80 − 1 = ☐
70 − 1 = ☐
60 − 1 = ☐

4 25 − 10 = 15
26 − 10 = ☐
27 − 10 = ☐

15 − 10 = ☐
25 − 10 = ☐
35 − 10 = ☐

50 − 1 = ☐
40 − 1 = ☐
30 − 1 = ☐

Think like a mathematician

1 more means the same as +1.
10 more means the same as +10.
1 less means the same as −1.
10 less means the same as −10.

Try this

Julio buys 37 sweets.
Nina buys 10 fewer
sweets than Julio.
How many sweets did
Nina buy?

Self-check

A Number to 100

1 Write the missing numbers.

2 Continue the patterns.

a Count in twos.
40, 42, 44,

____, ____, ____

b Count in fives.
20, 25, 30,

____, ____, ____

1	2	3	4	5	6	7	8	9	10
11	12	13	14	15	16	17	18	19	20
21	22		24	25	26	27	28	29	30
31	32	33		35	36	37	38	39	40
41	42	43	44		46	47	48	49	50
51	52	53	54	55		57	58	59	60
61	62	63	64	65	66		68	69	70
71	72	73	74	75	76	77	78	79	80
81	82	83	84	85	86	87	88	89	90
91	92	93	94	95	96	97	98	99	100

B Comparing and rounding numbers

1 Draw a picture of a train with five carriages.
The 1st carriage is blue. The 2nd carriage is red.
The 3rd carriage has 3 windows. The 4th carriage has a person waving from the window. The 5th carriage is green.

2 Round these numbers to the nearest multiple of 10.
a 18 ⟶ ☐   b ☐ ⟵ 81

3 Copy the number line and write the missing numbers.

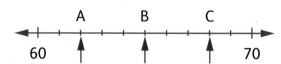

C Number and place value

1 How many tens are there in each number?
a 29   b 39   c 49   d 58   e 57   f 56

2 How many ones are there in each number?
a 59   b 69   c 79   d 23   e 24   f 25

3 Julio is 7 years old. Mia is 1 year younger. How old is Mia?

Unit 2   Geometry and problem solving

2a 2-D shapes and symmetry

Explore

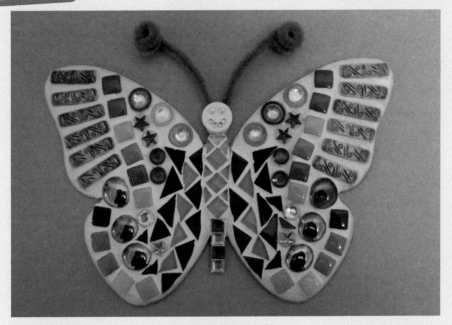

What shapes can you see?

Key words

symmetrical
line of symmetry
2-D shape
corner
side
circle
triangle
square
rectangle
pentagon
hexagon
oval
semi-circle

2-D shapes and their properties

Learn

Here is one way to sort the shapes.

Shapes that have 4 corners	Shapes that do not have 4 corners

Can you sort the shapes in another way?

Practise

1 Choose a different way to sort these shapes into two groups.

a

semi-circle   circle

triangle   rectangle

pentagon   oval

b

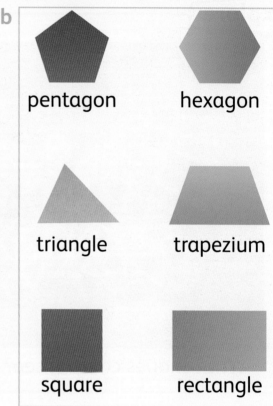

pentagon   hexagon

triangle   trapezium

square   rectangle

Try this

Write two headings for the table.

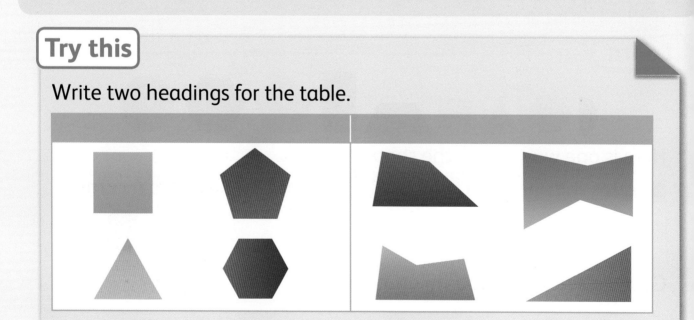

Drawing a line of symmetry

Learn

Symmetrical means that something is the same on two or more sides.

A line of symmetry shows that the shape or picture is symmetrical.

Fold the shape down the line of symmetry. The shape is the same on both sides.

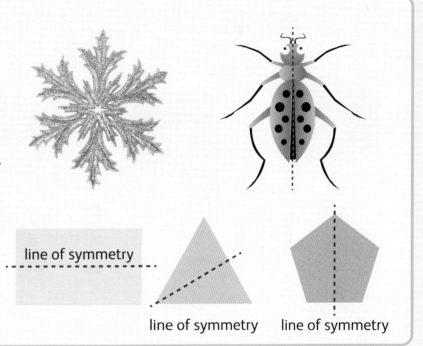

line of symmetry

line of symmetry   line of symmetry

Practise

1 Copy the shapes.
   Then draw a line of symmetry.

2 Copy the table. Draw four shapes in each box.

Shapes with lines of symmetry	Shapes with no lines of symmetry

3 Make a symmetrical pattern.

Try this

All rectangles have a line of symmetry.

Is Zara correct?
Explain your answer.

2b Shapes around me

Explore

Remember the difference between 2-D and 3-D shapes!

Name the 2-D and 3-D shapes you can see.

Learn

A 3-D shape is a solid shape.

Cube	Sphere
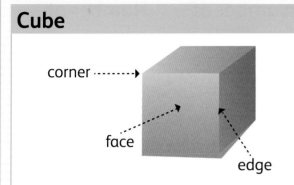	
A cube has 6 faces, 8 corners and 12 edges.	A sphere has 1 curved surface, 0 corners and 0 edges.

Square-based pyramid	Triangular prism
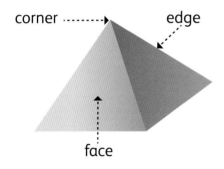	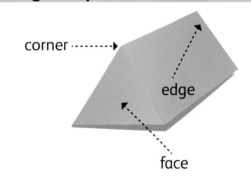
A square-based pyramid has 5 faces, 5 corners and 8 edges.	A triangular prism has 5 faces, 6 corners and 9 edges.

What shapes are the faces of this triangular-based pyramid?

The faces are 2-D shapes.

A triangular-based pyramid has 4 triangles as its faces.

Practise

1 Copy and complete. The first one has been done for you.

Shape	Number of corners	Number of faces	Number of edges
Cylinder	0	3	2
Cuboid			
Triangular-based prism			
Triangular-based pyramid			

2 What 2-D shapes are the faces of these 3-D shapes?

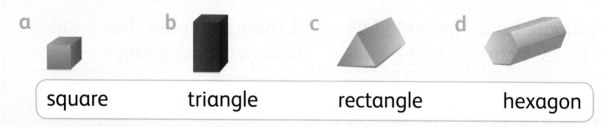

a   b   c   d

| square | triangle | rectangle | hexagon |

Try this

Look at the shapes around you. Write a list of five 2-D shapes and five 3-D shapes. Which shape is the most common?

Self-check

A 2-D shapes and symmetry

1 Which 2-D shapes is the robot made of?

2 a How many sides does each shape have?

b How many corners does each shape have?

3 Choose one of the shapes. Copy it.
Draw a line of symmetry on the shape.

B Shapes around me

1    2

a Write the name of each 3-D shape.

b How many faces does each shape have?

c How many edges does each shape have?

d How many corners does each shape have?

e Which 2-D shapes are the faces and curved surfaces on each 3-D shape?

⏻ 3a　Number facts

Explore

Match the numbers to make a total of 10.

$2 + \boxed{} = 10$　　　$\boxed{} + 6 = 10$

$10 = 2 + \boxed{}$　　　$10 = \boxed{} + 6$

What other totals can you make?

Which child could sit on the see-saw to balance it?

$9 + 1 = 3 + \boxed{}$

Key words ⏻

add

subtract

multiple

multiply

total

partition

Learn

We can partition 14 counters in different ways.

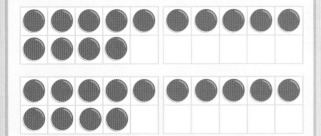

Write other ways to partition 14 counters.

Look at the related facts:

$3 + 11 = 14$ $14 - 11 = 3$
$11 + 3 = 14$ $14 - 3 = 11$

Practise

1 Use tens frames and counters to make 13 in different ways. Write the number sentences.

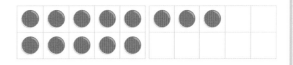

2 Copy and complete the related facts.

$16 = 9 + 7$	$12 = 4 + 8$
$16 = \square + 9$	$12 = \square + 4$
$16 - 9 = \square$	$12 - 4 = \square$
$16 - 7 = \square$	$12 - \square = 4$

$16 = 11 + 5$	$12 = 10 + 2$
$\square = 5 + 11$	$\square = 2 + 10$
$16 - 11 = \square$	$12 - 10 = \square$
$16 - \square = 11$	$\square - 2 = 10$

$19 = 12 + 7$	$19 - 12 = \square$
$19 = \square + 12$	$\square - 7 = 12$

Try this

Write five sets of two items to balance the scales.

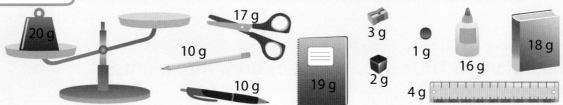

20 g   17 g   3 g   18 g
10 g   1 g   16 g
10 g   19 g   2 g
4 g

Totals to 100

Learn

We can use number facts up to 10 to help add multiples of 10.

1 + 9 = 10

10 + 90 = 100

Practise

1 Copy and complete.

a 10 + 90 = ☐
   20 + 80 = ☐
   40 + 60 = ☐

b 50 + ☐ = 100
   70 + ☐ = 100
   100 + ☐ = 100

c 100 − ☐ = 90
   100 − ☐ = 70
   100 − ☐ = 50

2 Explain how you can work out 30 + 70 mentally.

3 Copy and complete the related facts for each number sentence.
  An example has been done for you.

a 40 + 60 = 100
   60 + 40 = 100
   100 − 60 = 40
   100 − 40 = 60

b 30 + 70 = 100
   ☐ + 30 = 100
   100 − ☐ = 30
   ☐ − 30 = 70

c 20 + 80 = 100
   ☐ + ☐ = 100
   100 − ☐ = ☐
   100 − ☐ = ☐

Try this

A farmer planted 100 seeds. 80 seeds grew into plants.
How many did not grow?

⏻ 3b Addition and subtraction

Explore

Key words ⏻
addition
subtraction
equal
double
number facts

Rafael is playing a game. He throws the bean bags into three buckets with numbers on them. He has three bean bags.

What different scores could he get?

Learn

You can add numbers in any order.

3 + 2 = 2 + 3

When adding sets of numbers, look for number bonds to 10 or doubles.

Learn your number bonds to 10 and your doubles!

1 + 9	6 + 4	1 + 1 = 2	6 + 6 = 12
2 + 8	7 + 3	2 + 2 = 4	7 + 7 = 14
3 + 7	8 + 2	3 + 3 = 6	8 + 8 = 16
4 + 6	9 + 1	4 + 4 = 8	9 + 9 = 18
5 + 5	10 + 0	5 + 5 = 10	

For example:

3 + 4 + 3 + 6 = ☐

Can you spot any doubles?

That is right! Double 3 = 3 + 3 = 6

Can you spot any number bonds to 10?

That is right! 4 + 6 = 10

So 3 + 4 + 3 + 6 = 16

double 3 = 6

③ + 4 + ③ + 6 = 16

4 + 6 = 10

Practise

1 Copy the numbers and add. Write the answers.

An example has been done for you.   3 + 4 + 4 + 2 = 13

3 + 2 + 8 + 3 =	4 + 3 + 7 + 4 =	1 + 2 + 2 + 9 =	1 + 4 + 9 + 4 =
4 + 2 + 8 + 4 =	5 + 3 + 7 + 5 =	2 + 2 + 2 + 8 =	2 + 4 + 8 + 4 =
5 + 2 + 8 + 5 =	6 + 3 + 7 + 6 =	3 + 2 + 2 + 7 =	3 + 4 + 7 + 4 =
6 + 2 + 8 + 6 =	7 + 3 + 7 + 7 =	4 + 2 + 2 + 6 =	4 + 4 + 6 + 4 =

2 The children are playing a game.
They knock over the skittles with a ball.
Who has the highest score?

Name	Throw				Total score
	1st	2nd	3rd	4th	
Carlos	4	2	6	2	
Sofia	6	6	3	7	
Lola	3	3	1	9	
Dylan	2	8	4	4	
Almaa	5	5	3	7	
Matias	1	1	6	4	

3 Tessa is playing a game. She throws
3 balls at the target. What can her
score be?

Write some of the
possible combinations.

3
5
7

Try this

$\square + 2 + \square = 8$

Think like a mathematician

We can add numbers in any order. We
cannot subtract numbers in any order.
Why not?

Add and subtract one-digit and two-digit numbers

Learn

Addition:

32 + 4 = 36

- Remember that you can do addition in any order!
- Put the bigger number in your head (32).
- Count on the smaller number (4).

Subtraction:

27 − 3 = 24

- Always do subtraction in the order it appears.
- Put the first number in your head (27).
- Count back the other number (3).

You can use a number line.

- Write the bigger number at the beginning of the number line.
- Add the smaller number.

Count on 4.

You can use a number line.

- Write the first number at the end of the number line.
- Subtract the smaller number.

Count back 3.

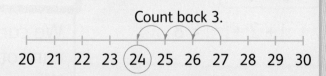

Practise

1 Copy the calculations. Write the answers.
The first one has been done for you.

a 59 – 1 = 58   b 61 + 1 = ☐   c 73 + 1 = ☐   d 87 – 1 = ☐
   59 – 2 = ☐   61 + 2 = ☐   73 + 2 = ☐   87 – 2 = ☐
   59 – 3 = ☐   61 + 3 = ☐   73 + 3 = ☐   87 – 3 = ☐
   59 – 4 = ☐   61 + 4 = ☐   73 + 4 = ☐   87 – 4 = ☐

2 Choose two number cards.

| 21 | 33 | 42 | 51 | 62 |

Write an addition calculation. Use the two numbers you have chosen.

Solve the calculation.

3 Choose two number cards.

| 29 | 38 | 47 | 56 | 69 |

Write a subtraction calculation. Use the two numbers you have chosen.

Solve the calculation.

Try this

Rashid thought of a number. He took away 5. He had 41 left.

What was his number?

3c Multiplication

Explore

Flamingos are pink birds. They sometimes stand on one leg.

How many flamingos do you think Manjil has spotted?

Key words

multiplication
array
multiples
repeated addition
times
lots of

Repeated addition and arrays

2 multiplied by 3 means 2, three times.
We can show this as an array.

We can write this as repeated addition: 2 + 2 + 2 = 6

			Array	Repeated addition
2	×	3	=	2 + 2 + 2

size of group   number of groups

Here are more examples:

2 × 1 = 2

2 × 2 = 4   2 + 2 = 4

2 × 3 = 6   2 + 2 + 2 = 6

2 × 4 = 8   2 + 2 + 2 + 2 = 8

2 × 5 = 10   2 + 2 + 2 + 2 + 2 = 10

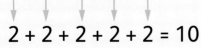

2 + 2 + 2 + 2 + 2 = 10

1 Write a multiplication calculation for each array.

a  b  c 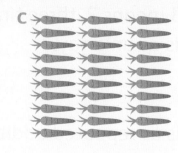 d

2 Make an array for each calculation.

a	b	c
2 × 1	5 × 1	10 × 1
2 × 2	5 × 2	10 × 2
2 × 3	5 × 3	10 × 3
2 × 4	5 × 4	10 × 4

3 Write a repeated addition for each calculation.

a	b	c
2 × 5	5 × 5	10 × 5
2 × 6	5 × 6	10 × 6
2 × 7	5 × 7	10 × 7
2 × 8	5 × 8	10 × 8

4 Write a number calculation. Then draw an array for each problem.

An owl catches 5 mice each night.
How many mice does she catch …

a in 5 nights?

b in 6 nights?

c in 1 week?

Try this

Choose two single-digit numbers.
Write a multiplication calculation.
Draw an array.

Multiples of 2, 5 and 10

Learn

Practise counting in twos, fives and tens.

| 2 | 4 | 6 | 8 | 10 | 12 | 14 | 16 | 8 | 20 |

| 5 | 10 | 15 | 20 | 25 | 30 | 35 | 40 | 45 | 50 |

| 10 | 20 | 30 | 40 | 50 | 60 | 70 | 80 | 90 | 100 |

Multiples of 2 are all even numbers. They can be divided by 2.
Multiples of 5 end in the digits 5 or 0. They can be divided by 5.
Multiples of 10 end in the digit 0. They can be divided by 10.

Practise

1 Count the caterpillar's legs. Write the numbers that are multiples of 2.

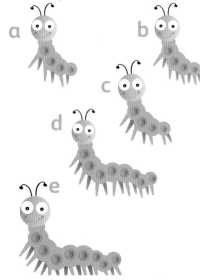

2 Count the lemons on each tree. Write the numbers that are multiples of 5.

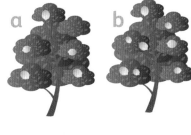

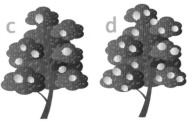

3 Write the numbers that are multiples of 10.

14 40 18 80 25 20 60 100

Learn

Solve the problem.

Chef can buy flour in 5 kg bags and in 10 kg bags. He needs 35 kg of flour.
How many bags could he buy?

10 kg bag (blue bag)	5 kg bag (white bag)	Total
10 × 0 = 0	5 × 7 = 35	0 + 35 = 35 kg
10 × 1 = 10	5 × 5 = 25	10 + 25 = 35 kg
10 × 2 = 20	5 × 3 = 15	20 + 15 = 35 kg
10 × 3 = 30	5 × 1 = 5	30 + 5 = 35 kg

What are the possible combinations?

[ ] blue bags and [ ] white bags.

Practise

1 Sugar is sold in 5 kg bags and 10 kg bags.
   The chef needs 45 kg of sugar.
   What combinations of bags could he buy?

2 Eggs are sold in boxes of 5 or boxes of 10.
   The chef needs 55 eggs.
   What combination of boxes could he buy?

3 Oranges are sold in bags of 5 or boxes of 10.
   The chef needs 65 oranges.
   What combinations of bags and boxes could he buy?

Can you help the chef with his shopping?

Self-check

A Number facts

1 How many different ways can you make 10 using the numbers you can see?

Self-check

2 Copy and complete.

20 – 10 = ☐   20 – 3 = ☐

20 – 5 = ☐   20 – 7 = ☐

20 – 9 = ☐   20 – 2 = ☐

20 – 4 = ☐   20 – 6 = ☐

20 – 8 = ☐   20 – 1 = ☐

3 100 passengers boarded an aeroplane. 30 were carrying a suitcase. How many were not carrying a suitcase?

100 – 30 = ☐

B Addition and subtraction

1 Choose four numbers from 1 to 10. Add the numbers together.

2 Copy and complete.

1 ☐ 6 = 7   10 ☐ 8 = 2   4 ☐ 5 = 9

8 ☐ 6 = 2   6 ☐ 8 = 14   5 ☐ 4 = 1

3 There were 34 goats on the mountain. Two more goats arrived. How many goats are there on the mountain now?

C Multiplication

1 Write a multiplication calculation to match each array.

a   b

2 The baker packs bread rolls into bags.
Each bag has 4 rolls.

a How many rolls are there in 2 bags?

b How many rolls are there in 5 bags?

c How many rolls are there in 10 bags?

4a Money

Key words
dollar
cent
coins
notes
change
pay

Explore

Renata and Kadir each have $20 to spend.
What items can they buy?

Making different amounts

Learn

These are the coins and notes we use.

We can make any amount using these coins and notes.

 = 3c

= 13c

= $13

Calculating change

Learn

When we pay for things with money we often get money back. This is called 'change'.

For example:

Kadir buys a kite. It cost $17.
He pays with a $20 note.

$20 – $17 = ☐

These numbers are close together.
We can find the difference. Put the smaller number in your head. Count on.

Kadir counts on 3.
$20 – $17 = $3
He needs $3 change.

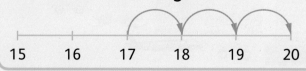

15   16   17   18   19   20

Practise

1 How much money is there? Write each total.

a (1¢) (5¢)   b (1¢) (5¢) (10¢)

c (25¢) (10¢) (5¢)   d (25¢) (10¢) (5¢) (1¢)

e [$ 1 $] [$ 1 $] [$ 5 $]   f [$ 1 $] [$ 1 $] [$ 1 $] [$ 5 $]

2 Pay with the exact amount for these items.
Which coins and notes could you use?

$11

$14

$13

$10

3 You pay for each item with a $20 note.
How much change do you get?

$18

$16

$14

$15

$17

Try this

Which two items could Matias buy with $15
and still have change?

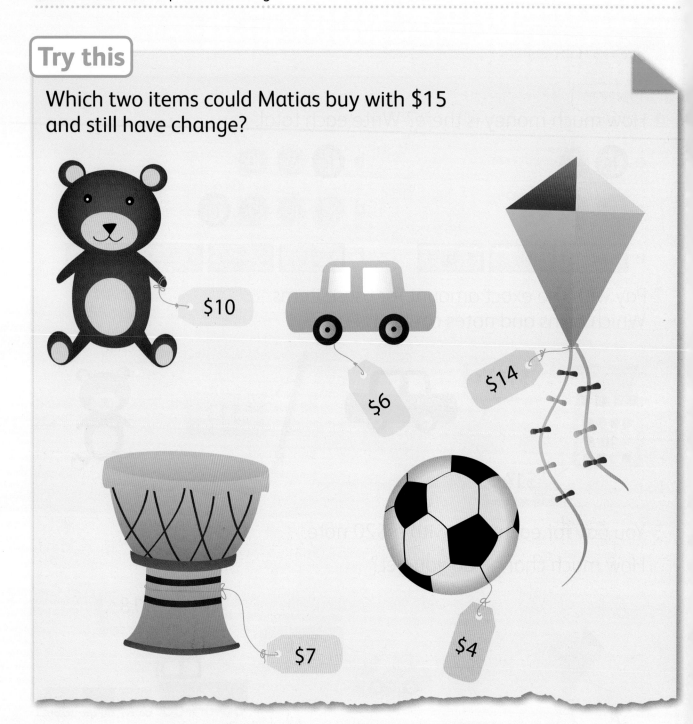

$10

$6

$14

$7

$4

Think like a mathematician

Use your number bonds and number
facts to 15 to help you.
15 − 6 = 9 $15 − $9 = $6

4b Measuring length

Explore

I think I can jump about 60 metres.

Mark

Mark

cm
0 10 20 30 40 50 60 70 80

I think I can jump about 60 cm.

Carla

Carla

cm
0 10 20 30 40 50 60 70 80

Key words
centimetre
metre
estimate
length
compare
longest
shortest
tallest
furthest

Who made a good estimate?

How far did both children jump?

Who jumped the furthest?

Using non-standard and standard units to measure

Learn

Using non-standard units

How many counters fit along the pencil?

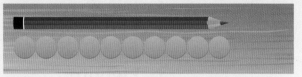

The pencil is 10 counters long.

Using centimetres and a ruler

The tip of the pencil is in line with the 12. The pencil is 12 cm long.

Non-standard units are all different.

Practise

1 Estimate and then measure how many counters long each item is.

    book   hand span   shoe

2 Estimate and then measure how many centimetres long each item is.

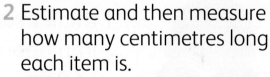

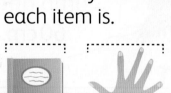 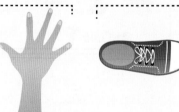

    book   hand span   shoe

3 Estimate and then measure how far you can jump.

Comparing lengths

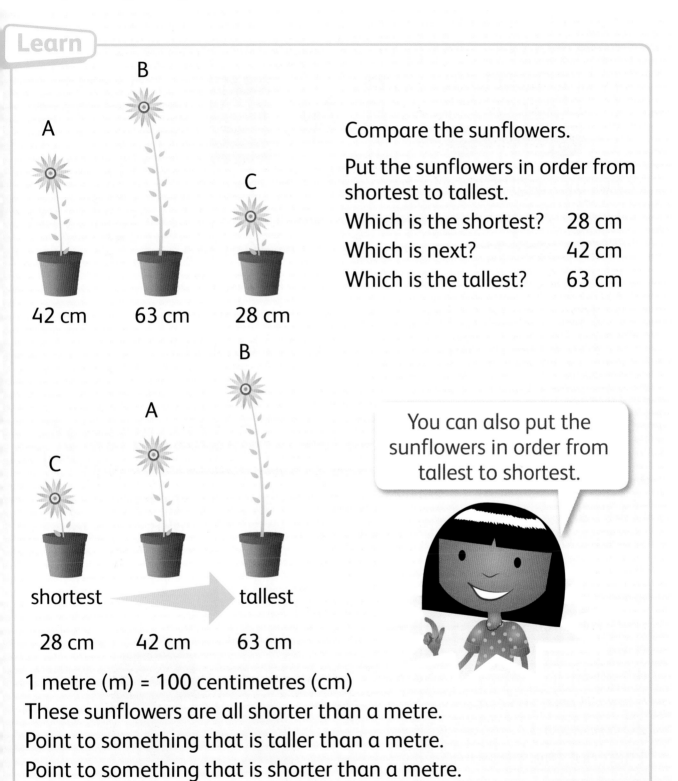

Compare the sunflowers.

Put the sunflowers in order from shortest to tallest.

Which is the shortest?   28 cm

Which is next?   42 cm

Which is the tallest?   63 cm

You can also put the sunflowers in order from tallest to shortest.

1 metre (m) = 100 centimetres (cm)

These sunflowers are all shorter than a metre.

Point to something that is taller than a metre.

Point to something that is shorter than a metre.

Practise

1 Estimate which items are taller or longer than a metre.

   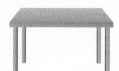

2 Put the lengths in order from shortest to longest.
   Use a ruler and metre stick to compare.

   a 4 cm, 8 cm, 6 cm   b 1 m, 10 m, 5 m

   c 18 cm, 16 cm, 14 cm   d 10 m, 20 m, 15 m

   e 24 cm, 28 cm, 26 cm   f 20 m, 30 m, 25 m

   g 34 cm, 38 cm, 36 cm   h 35 m, 40 m, 3 m

Try this

You will need

- string
- a pair of scissors
- a ruler

Measure the string using a ruler. Cut the pieces to these lengths:
5 cm, 10 cm, 15 cm, 20 cm, 25 cm

Then put the measures in order from shortest to longest.

Think like a mathematician

Place the 0 on the ruler at the beginning of the object you are measuring.

Pull the string or ribbon straight before you measure it.

4c Time

Explore

What different type of clocks can you see?

What are the times on all the clocks in the picture?

Key words
time
year
month
week
hour
minute
second
half an hour

Telling the time

Learn

 What time is it?

The hour hand is pointing to the 4.

The minute hand is pointing to the 12.

It is 4 o'clock.

On a digital clock this is:

 What time is it?

The hour hand is pointing past the 8.

The minute hand is pointing to the 6.

It is half past 8.

On a digital clock this is:

Practise

1 What time is it?

a    b

c    d

2 What time is it?

a   b

c    b

3 What time is it?

a  2:00

b  5:00

c  2:30

d  6:30

Ordering time

Learn

Do you remember the days of the week?

Saturday Sunday Monday
Friday
Thursday Wednesday Tuesday

Do you remember the months of the year?

October November December
September January
August February
July June May April March

There are 7 days in a week.
There are 24 hours in a day.
There are 60 minutes in an hour.
There are 60 seconds in a minute.

There are 12 months in a year.

Practise

1 Write the days of the week in order.

| Wednesday | Saturday | Friday | Sunday |

| Tuesday | Thursday | Monday |

2 Write the months of the year in order.

| March | April | January | November |

| February | August | May | July |

| December | June | October | September |

3 Copy and complete the sentences.

☐ hours in a day   ☐ months in a year

July						
Sun	Mon	Tues	Wed	Thu	Fri	Sat
						1
2	3	4	5	6	7	8
9	10	11	12	13	14	15
16	17	18	19	20	21	22
23	24	25	26	27	28	29
30	31					

_____ is the month after August.   _____ is the month before February.

Friday is after Thursday.   _____ is after Friday.

Monday is before Tuesday.   _____ is before Saturday.

Try this

Sofia goes on holiday on Monday. She will be away for three days. On which day of the week will she return?

1 hour = 60 minutes
1 minute = 60 seconds

Think like a mathematician

- The short hand on a clock counts the hours.
- The long hand on a clock counts the minutes.

Self-check

A Money

1 Lola bought a kite for $8. Which coins or notes could she use to pay?

2 Dylan bought a toy train for $9. He paid with a $20 note. How much change did he get?

B Measuring length

1 Put these lengths in order from shortest to longest.
a 3 cm, 9 cm, 12 cm, 6 cm
b 13 m, 19 m, 22 m, 16 m
c 23 cm, 29 cm, 32 cm, 26 cm

2 How long is the piece of ribbon?

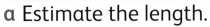

a Estimate the length.
b Then measure it with a ruler.

C Time

1 What time is it?

2 Which day comes after Saturday?
Which month comes after March?

Unit 5   Problem solving and review

5a Under the sea

Problem 1

a How many blue fish are there?

b How many spotted fish are there?

c How many orange fish are there?

d How many blue, spotted and orange fish are there altogether?

e How many more orange fish are there than blue fish?

Problem 2

There are 10 fish in the bucket. They are numbered from 1 to 10.

Ernesto catches 3 fish.
His fish have these numbers:

3 + 7 + 2 = 12
Ernesto's total is 12.

Bonita catches 3 fish. She catches and .

a What number could the third fish have?

b What could her total be?

Problem 3

Look at the picture.
This type of fish always has three spots that are orange, blue and white.
But the spots can be in different combinations.
Which fish is not a correct combination?

a   **b**   **c**

Draw two more correct combinations.

Problem 4

The diver recorded the number of different fish he saw.

Fish	Tally	Number of fish
Pink fish	ЖЖЖ ЖЖЖ	
Blue fish	ЖЖЖ ЖЖЖ Ж	
Spotty fish	‖	
Striped fish	‖‖	
Yellow fish	‖‖	
Stingray	‖	

1 Write the total the diver saw.

a How many ⬛ and ◗ ?

b How many ⬛ and ◉ ?

c How many ⬛ and ◗ ?

d How many ⬛ and ◗ ?

e How many ⬛ and ◗ ?

f How many ⬛ and ◉ ?

g How many ⬛ and ◗ ?

h How many ⬛ and ◗ ?

> We use tally marks to count fives: ЖЖ

2 The diver tagged some fish.
   a There were 28 orange fish. The diver tagged 3.
     How many did he not tag?
   b There were 36 red fish. The diver tagged 5.
     How many did he not tag?
   c There were 19 silver fish. The diver tagged 6.
     How many did he not tag?

Problem 5

Rosi saw 30 blue fish and 6 purple fish.

Kai saw 7 more fish than Rosi.

How many fish did Kai see?

Problem 6

Rosi had enough oxygen to dive for 30 minutes.

Kai had enough oxygen to dive for 10 minutes longer than Rosi.

Garon had enough oxygen to dive for 5 minutes less than Kai.

For how long could Garon dive?

6a Counting patterns

Explore

How much does the fruit cost?

Choose some fruit for your basket.
How much does your basket of fruit cost?

Counting in tens

Learn

1	2	3	4	5	6	7	8	9	10
11	12	13	14	15	16	17	18	19	20
21	22	23	24	25	26	27	28	29	30
31	32	33	34	35	36	37	38	39	40
41	42	43	44	45	46	47	48	49	50
51	52	53	54	55	56	57	58	59	60
61	62	63	64	65	66	67	68	69	70
71	72	73	74	75	76	77	78	79	80
81	82	83	84	85	86	87	88	89	90
91	92	93	94	95	96	97	98	99	100

counting on

counting back

Count on in tens from 23.
Find 23. Add 10 each time.

Count back in tens from 98.
Find 98. Subtract 10 each time.

Find the pattern.
What do you notice?

Practise

1 Count on in tens. The first one has been done for you.

a 24, 34, 44, 54, 64, 74, 84

b 25, ___, ___, ___, ___, ___, ___

c 26, ___, ___, ___, ___, ___, ___

d 27, ___, ___, ___, ___, ___, ___

e 28, ___, ___, ___, ___, ___, ___

2 Count back in tens.

a 97, ___, ___, ___, ___, ___, ___

b 96, ___, ___, ___, ___, ___, ___

c 95, ___, ___, ___, ___, ___, ___

d 94, ___, ___, ___, ___, ___, ___

e 93, ___, ___, ___, ___, ___, ___

Try this

Jade is 10 cm shorter than Rashid. How tall is Jade?

Macie is 10 cm taller than Rashid. How tall is Macie?

Jade   Rashid   Macie
86 cm

Problem solving

Learn

How many buttons are there altogether?

Each robot has 5 buttons.

Count in fives.

5, 10, 15, 20, 25, 30

There are 30 buttons.

How many fingers are there altogether?

Each robot has 10 fingers.

Count in tens.

10, 20, 30, 40, 50, 60

There are 60 fingers.

Practise

1 Take a pile of counters.

Arrange and then count them …

a in twos.

b in fives.

c in tens.

How many are there?

2 There are 10 people in each basket.

How many people are there …

a in 3 hot air balloons?

b in 4 hot air balloons?

c in 5 hot air balloons?

d in 6 hot air balloons?

3 Each bicycle has 2 wheels.

How many wheels are there …

a on 3 bicycles?

b on 4 bicycles?

c on 5 bicycles?

d on 6 bicycles?

4 Each flower has 5 petals.

How many petals are there …

a on 3 flowers?

b on 4 flowers?

c on 5 flowers?

d on 6 flowers?

Think like a mathematician

Look at a 100 square. What patterns can you see when counting in twos, fives and tens?

6b Comparing, ordering and estimating

Explore

These numbers are in order.
What is the biggest number?
What is the smallest number?
What number could the shirt on the ground be?

Key words

compare
order
estimate

Ordering numbers

Learn

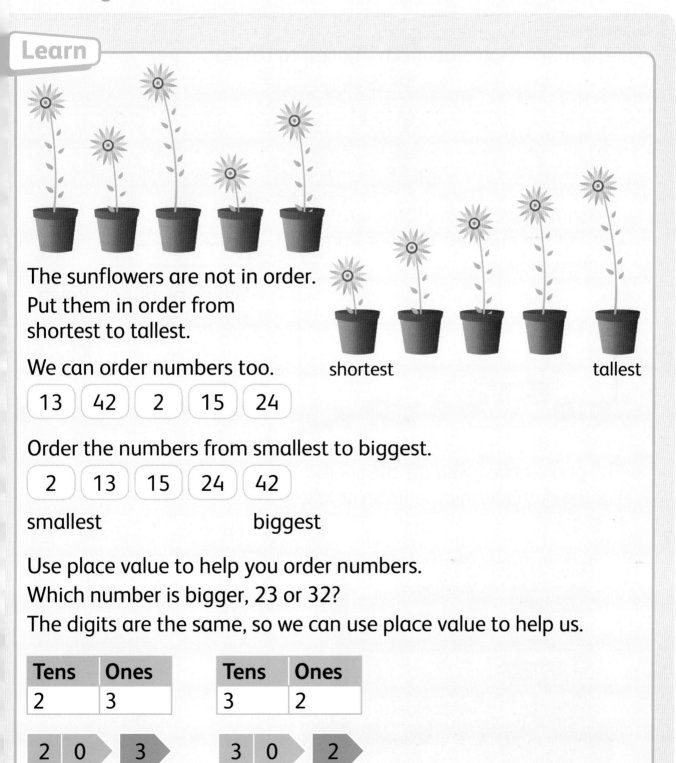

The sunflowers are not in order.
Put them in order from shortest to tallest.

shortest   tallest

We can order numbers too.

| 13 | 42 | 2 | 15 | 24 |

Order the numbers from smallest to biggest.

| 2 | 13 | 15 | 24 | 42 |

smallest   biggest

Use place value to help you order numbers.
Which number is bigger, 23 or 32?
The digits are the same, so we can use place value to help us.

Tens	Ones
2	3

Tens	Ones
3	2

2 0 3   3 0 2

Practise

Put the numbers in order from smallest to biggest.

1 a 8, 7, 4, 9, 1
   b 2, 10, 3, 6, 9
   c 5, 2, 1, 4, 8

2 a 25, 16, 14, 52, 3
   b 4, 26, 62, 17, 15
   c 72, 27, 5, 18, 16

3 a 11, 16, 61, 39, 35
   b 34, 12, 38, 26, 62
   c 33, 37, 13, 63, 36

4 The shirts have fallen off the washing line. Put the numbers in order from smallest to biggest.

5 The books have fallen off the shelf. Put the numbers in order from smallest to biggest.

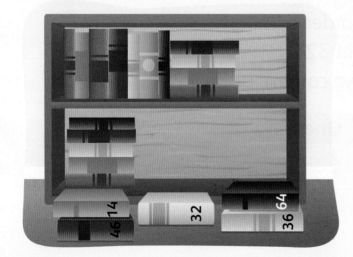

Try this

Which plant has grown the tallest?

a   b   c   d   e

Put the pictures in order from tallest to shortest.

1st ☐   2nd ☐

3rd ☐   4th ☐

5th ☐

Comparing numbers

Learn

We can use > and < to compare numbers too.

 3 < 4

 4 > 3

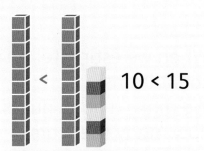 < 10 < 15

10 is smaller than 15.
Now you can show
that 15 > 10.

3 is smaller than 4.   4 is bigger than 3.

Practise

Copy and complete the number sentences. Use the < or > signs. The first one has been done for you.

1
a 20 < 29
b 31 ◯ 38
c 27 ◯ 22
d 36 ◯ 33
e 45 ◯ 41

2
a 99 ◯ 98
b 98 ◯ 97
c 96 ◯ 97
d 95 ◯ 96
e 94 ◯ 95

3 Solve the problem.

a Do the nuts in bag B weigh 60 g or 40 g? Explain your answer.
b Copy and complete to match the picture.
50 g < ☐

Try this

19   28   37   46   55

Use the number cards and the < or > signs to make number sentences. An example is 19 < 28.

How many different number sentences can you make?

Estimating numbers

Learn

When we estimate, we do not count items.
We make a good guess about how many there are.
Estimate how many pencils are in the container.
There are ____ pencils.

> I estimate there are 20 pencils in the container.

Practise

1   A   B   C

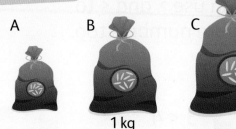

1 kg

a Estimate how many kilograms of rice there are in bag A.

b Estimate how many kilograms of rice there are in bag C.

2   A   B   C

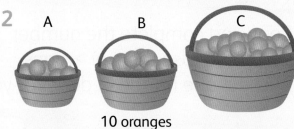

10 oranges

a Estimate how many oranges there are in basket A.

b Estimate how many oranges there are in basket B.

Try this

Fill a container with counters. Estimate how many counters are in the container. Ask your partner to estimate.
Now count the counters. Who made the closest estimate?

6c Number and place value

Explore

It takes me 26 minutes to get to school.

It takes me 6 minutes to get to school.

Gabriela

Miguel

Key words
digit
tens
ones
partition

How long does it take you to get to school?

It takes Gabriela 8 minutes to cycle to school.
It takes Miguel 10 minutes longer to walk to school.
How long does it take Miguel to get to school?

Partitioning

Learn

$$17 = 10 + 7$$

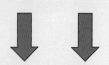

$$27 = 20 + 7$$

Practise

Partition the numbers. The first one has been done for you.

a 37 = 30 + 7

b 47 = ____ + ____

c 57 = ____ + ____

d 67 = ____ + ____

e 77 = ____ + ____

f 87 = ____ + ____

g 18 = ____ + ____

h 28 = ____ + ____

i 38 = ____ + ____

j 48 = ____ + ____

k 58 = ____ + ____

l 68 = ____ + ____

m 94 = ____ + ____

n 85 = ____ + ____

o 76 = ____ + ____

p 67 = ____ + ____

q 58 = ____ + ____

r 49 = ____ + ____

Use place value apparatus to make the numbers first!

Try this

Use a spinner to make a two-digit number.

Repeat five times.

Put the numbers in order from biggest to smallest.

More and less

1 more is the same as adding 1.
1 more than 14 is 15.
$14 + 1 = 15$

```
├──┼──┼──┼──⌒┼──┼──┼──┼──┼──┤
10  11  12  13  14  15  16  17  18  19  20
```

10 more is the same as adding 10.
10 more than 14 is 24.
$14 + 10 = 24$

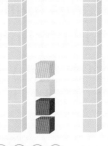

```
├──┼──┼──┼──⌒⌒⌒⌒⌒⌒⌒⌒⌒⌒─┤
10 11 12 13 14 15 16 17 18 19 20 21 22 23 24 25
```

1 less is the same as subtracting 1.
1 less than 14 is 13.
$14 - 1 = 13$

```
├──┼──┼──⌒┼──┼──┼──┼──┼──┼──┤
10  11  12  13  14  15  16  17  18  19  20
```

10 less is the same as subtracting 10.
10 less than 14 is 4.
$14 - 10 = 4$

```
├──┼──┼──⌒⌒⌒⌒⌒⌒⌒⌒⌒⌒─┤
1  2  3  4  5  6  7  8  9  10  11  12  13  14  15
```

Copy and complete the calculations. Two have been done for you.

1		2		3		4	
a	44 + 1 = 45	a	89 − 1 = 88	a	61 + 10 = ☐	a	35 − 10 = ☐
b	45 + 1 = ☐	b	88 − 1 = ☐	b	62 + 10 = ☐	b	36 − 10 = ☐
c	46 + 1 = ☐	c	87 − 1 = ☐	c	63 + 10 = ☐	c	37 − 10 = ☐
d	38 + 1 = ☐	d	52 − 1 = ☐	d	64 − 10 = ☐	d	45 − 10 = ☐
e	48 + 1 = ☐	e	62 − 1 = ☐	e	74 − 10 = ☐	e	55 − 10 = ☐
f	58 + 1 = ☐	f	72 − 1 = ☐	f	84 − 10 = ☐	f	65 − 10 = ☐

Try this

Lucia, Carlos and Tania look for minibeasts. Lucia found 36.
Carlos found 1 more than Lucia.
Tania found 10 more than Carlos.
How many minibeasts did each learner find?

Think like a mathematician

Look at the number 35.
Remember the 3 has a value of 30.

Self-check

A Counting patterns

Maria, Victor and Amelie are growing plants with flowers. Each plant has five flowers.

1 Copy and complete the sentences.

Maria

   a Maria has ____ flowers.

   b Victor has 10 more flowers than Maria.
      Victor has ____ flowers.

   c Amelie has 1 less flower than Maria.
      Amelie has ____ flowers.

B Comparing, ordering and estimating

1

Name	Colour	Time
Farah		83 seconds
Sofia		86 seconds
Alec		85 seconds
Marlow		87 seconds
Bruno		84 seconds

a Who was 1st?   b Who was 2nd?   c Who was 3rd?

d What place did Bruno come?

e Copy the number sentences.
Write the sign < or > to complete them.

85 ◯ 86   83 ◯ 84   86 ◯ 85   84 ◯ 83

C Number and place value

1 a Look at the 100 square. Write down the missing numbers.

b Explain how you know which numbers are missing.

1	2	3	4	5	6	7	8	9	10
11	12	13	14	15	16	17	18	19	20
21	22	23	24	25	26		28	29	30
31	32	33	34	35	36	37	38	39	40
41		43	44	45	46	47	48	49	
51	52	53	54	55	56	57	58	59	60
61	62	63	64	65	66	67		69	70
71	72	73	74	75	76	77	78	79	80
81	82	83	84	85	86	87	88		90
91	92	93	94	95	96	97	98	99	100

7a Sorting objects and shapes

Explore

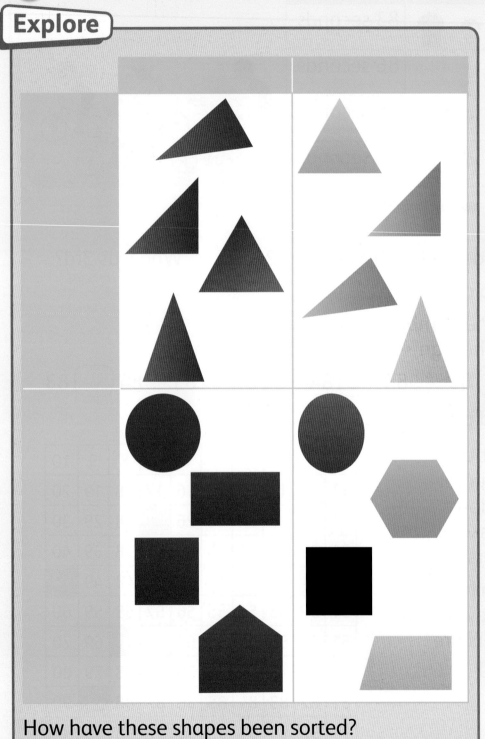

Key words

Carroll diagram
Venn diagram
multiple
odd
even
2-D shapes
circle
square
triangle
rectangle
pentagon
hexagon

How have these shapes been sorted?
What could the sorting labels be?

Venn diagrams and Carroll diagrams

Learn

We use Venn diagrams and Carroll diagrams for sorting numbers or objects. For example: 2, 6, 12, 14, 10, 20, 5, 15, 25, 35

Which numbers are even numbers? Which numbers are multiples of 5? The numbers have been sorted in these diagrams.

Venn diagram

even numbers   multiples of 5

6
2
12
14
10
20
5
25
15
35

Carroll diagram

	Even numbers	Not even numbers
Multiples of 5	10, 20	5, 15, 25, 35
Not multiples of 5	2, 6, 12, 14	

Where would the number 30 go? Where would the number 21 go? What do you notice about the two diagrams?

Practise

1 Copy and complete the Venn diagram.

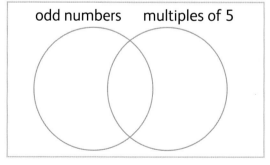

odd numbers   multiples of 5

5, 20, 3, 9, 7, 15, 10, 11, 25, 1

Try this

Choose a two-digit number. Put your number into a blank Venn diagram. Repeat.

Can your partner guess what your rule is?

7b Block graphs and pictograms

Explore

What is the most popular activity?
Which activity do you like best?

Key words

most
least
block graph
pictogram
tally
data

Tally chart

Fishing	IIII
In the sea	II<del>II</del>I
Flying a kite	III
Reading	II

Learn

Zara asked her friends what their favourite colour is.
She made a tally.

What is your favourite colour?

Blue	|||
Red	||||| ||
Orange	||
Green	||||

Record each person as a line. Remember the fifth line goes across the first four lines.

Zara used the data to draw a block graph and a pictogram.

A block graph to show children's favourite colours

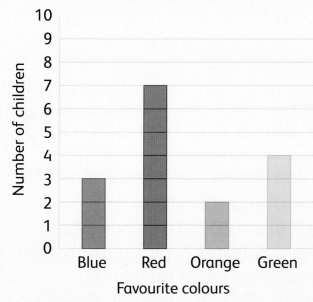

A pictogram to show favourite colours

Blue	👤👤👤
Red	👤👤👤👤👤👤👤
Orange	👤👤
Green	👤👤👤👤

Key: 👤 = 1 person

What is different about the pictogram and the graph?

77

Practise

Gabriel asked his friends what their favourite fruit is.

Fruit	Number of children
	II
	IIII
	JHT III
	I
	JHT

1 Write the totals.

2 Use your results to draw a block graph.

3 Answer these questions about the block graph.

   a How many children like mangoes?

   b How many children like oranges?

   c Which is the most popular fruit?

   d Which is the least popular fruit?

   e How many more children like oranges than mangoes?

   f How many children did Gabriel ask?

Try this

Ask your friends which is their favourite fruit.

a Choose four pieces of fruit.

b Record your friends' answers in a tally.

c Draw a block graph.

d Create a pictogram.

Think like a mathematician

When you collect data, remember to:
- Think of a question to ask.
- Think of answers to the question. Write down 4 or 5 different answers. One answer could be 'other'.
- The 5th mark in a tally goes across the other four marks.

Self-check

A Sorting objects and shapes

1 Copy the Carroll diagram.
   Choose 12 numbers to complete the diagram.

	20 or bigger	Not 20 or bigger
Even number		
Not an even number		

B Block graphs and pictograms

1 This tally chart shows children's favourite animals.

Animal	Tally
Elephant	卌 I
Zebra	卌 IIII
Rhino	III
Lion	卌 III

a Use the tally chart to draw a block graph.

b Write down the most popular animal.

c Write down the least popular animal.

d How many children like the lion the most?

e How many more children like the zebra than the rhino?

8a Addition and subtraction

Explore

Key words
add
subtract
digit
calculation

There are 86 people waiting for the train.
There is space for 10 people in each carriage.
There are 8 carriages.
How many people can ride on the train?

Adding and subtracting multiples of 10

Learn

1	2	3	4	5	6	7	8	9	10
11	12	13	14	15	16	17	18	19	20
21	22	23	24	25	26	27	28	29	30
31	32	33	34	35	36	37	38	39	40
41	42	43	44	45	46	47	48	49	50
51	52	53	54	55	56	57	58	59	60
61	62	63	64	65	66	67	68	69	70
71	72	73	74	75	76	77	78	79	80
81	82	83	84	85	86	87	88	89	90
91	92	93	94	95	96	97	98	99	100

$56 + 10 = 66$

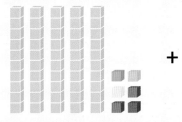 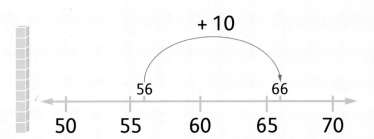

$56 - 10 = 46$

 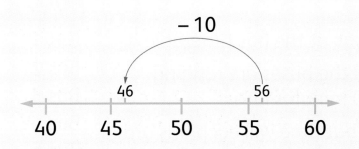

81

Practise

1 Partition each number into tens and ones. The first one has been done for you.

$(12) = (10) + (2)$

(23) (34) (45) (57) (66) (77) (88) (99)

2 Add or subtract multiples of 10. Two have been done for you.

$12 + 10 = \boxed{22}$	$22 + 40 = \Box$	$89 - 10 = \boxed{79}$	$99 - 50 = \Box$
$12 + 20 = \Box$	$22 + 50 = \Box$	$89 - 20 = \Box$	$99 - 60 = \Box$
$\Box = 12 + 30$	$\Box = 22 + 60$	$89 - 30 = \Box$	$99 - 70 = \Box$
$\Box = 12 + 40$	$\Box = 22 + 70$	$89 - 40 = \Box$	$99 - 80 = \Box$

3 Write the missing number. The first one has been done for you.

$36 - \boxed{10} = 26$	$36 + \Box = 46$	$45 - \Box = 35$	$45 + \Box = 55$
$36 - \Box = 16$	$36 + \Box = 56$	$45 - \Box = 25$	$45 + \Box = 65$
$36 - \Box = 6$	$36 + \Box = 66$	$45 - \Box = 15$	$45 + \Box = 75$

Try this

Look at the bus timetable.

All the buses are running
10 minutes late.

What time will each bus arrive?

Bus	Arrival time
Bus 1	1:05
Bus 2	1:15
Bus 3	1:25
Bus 4	1:35
Bus 5	1:45

Finding the difference between two near numbers

Learn

take-away   subtraction

–

find the difference   minus

> We can count back. Put the bigger number in your head. Count back with the smaller number. The answer is 19.

23 – 4 =

Use a number line. 23 – 4 = 19

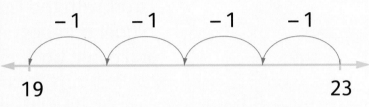

– 1   – 1   – 1   – 1

19   23

If two numbers are close together, we can count on to find the difference.

Which two numbers are close together?

45 – 9   89 – 3   23 – 4   15 – 13   64 – 23

Yes, you are right!   15 – 13

Put the smaller number in your head.

Count **up to** the bigger number.   We counted up two numbers.

13

15

15   14

The answer is 2.

Practise

1 Find the difference between the pairs that are close together.
The first one has been done for you.

a 13 ⟶ 15   2

b 56 ⟶ 59   c 36 ⟶ 39

d 71 ⟶ 74   e 45 ⟶ 47

f 94 ⟶ 98   g 62 ⟶ 65

2 Count back to solve these calculations.

29 − 3 = ☐	35 − 4 = ☐	86 − 2 = ☐
29 − 4 = ☐	35 − 3 = ☐	86 − 3 = ☐
29 − 5 = ☐	35 − 2 = ☐	86 − 4 = ☐
72 − 2 = ☐	53 − 3 = ☐	68 − 4 = ☐
72 − 3 = ☐	53 − 4 = ☐	68 − 3 = ☐
72 − 4 = ☐	53 − 5 = ☐	68 − 2 = ☐

Remember to start with the bigger number and count back.

3 Count on to solve these calculations.

27 − 26 = ☐	65 − 64 = ☐	18 − 17 = ☐
27 − 25 = ☐	65 − 63 = ☐	18 − 16 = ☐
27 − 24 = ☐	65 − 62 = ☐	18 − 15 = ☐
84 − 83 = ☐	53 − 52 = ☐	76 − 74 = ☐
84 − 82 = ☐	53 − 51 = ☐	76 − 73 = ☐
84 − 81 = ☐	53 − 50 = ☐	76 − 72 = ☐

Remember to start with the smaller number and count up.

4 Copy this table.

Counting on	Counting back
87 – 84	87 – 4

Choose the best method to solve each calculation below.
Then write the calculation in the correct column.

17 – 16   84 – 82   88 – 4   56 – 53   78 – 75

54 – 7   34 – 6   34 – 33   44 – 4   44 – 41

Try this

19 children were playing football in the park.
16 were girls.
How many were boys?

26 children were playing football in the park.
3 went home.
How many were left?

Remember to count on if the numbers are close together.

Remember to subtract if the numbers are far apart.

Think like a mathematician

- If the numbers are close together, find the difference by counting on.
- If the numbers are far apart, subtract the smaller number from the bigger number by counting back.

8b Multiplication

Explore

Monday

Tuesday

Wednesday

Thursday

Friday

Each day, Moussa caught twice as many fish as the day before.

How many fish did he catch on Thursday and Friday?

Key words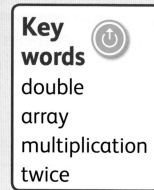

double
array
multiplication
twice

Doubles

Learn

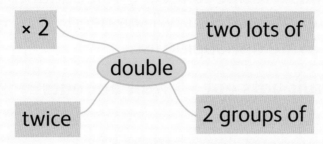

× 2   two lots of

double

twice   2 groups of

Double	Counters	As an addition	As a multiplication	As a division
Double 1		1 + 1 = 2	1 × 2 = 2	2 ÷ 2 = 1
Double 2		2 + 2 = 4	2 × 2 = 4	4 ÷ 2 = 2
Double 3		3 + 3 = 6	3 × 2 = 6	6 ÷ 2 = 3
Double 4		4 + 4 = 8	4 × 2 = 8	8 ÷ 2 = 4
Double 5		5 + 5 = 10	5 × 2 = 10	10 ÷ 2 = 5
Double 6		6 + 6 = 12	6 × 2 = 12	12 ÷ 2 = 6
Double 7		7 + 7 = 14	7 × 2 = 14	14 ÷ 2 = 7
Double 8		8 + 8 = 16	8 × 2 = 16	16 ÷ 2 = 8
Double 9		9 + 9 = 18	9 × 2 = 18	18 ÷ 2 = 9
Double 10		10 + 10 = 20	10 × 2 = 20	20 ÷ 2 = 10

Try to learn these doubles facts!

Practise

1 The zookeeper has a recipe to feed 1 fruit bat at the zoo.
How many pieces of each fruit will she need
for 2 fruit bats? Write a shopping list.

1 fruit bat eats	2 fruit bats eat	1 fruit bat eats	2 fruit bats eat
	☐ watermelons		☐ passion fruit
	☐ melons		☐ bananas
	☐ grapefruit		☐ kiwi fruit
	☐ plums		☐ mangoes
	☐ pineapples		☐ guavas

2 Copy these calculations. Add to find the total.

30 + 30 = ☐	☐ = 40 + 40	☐ = 15 + 15	10 + 10 = ☐
31 + 31 = ☐	☐ = 41 + 41	☐ = 25 + 25	11 + 11 = ☐
32 + 32 = ☐	☐ = 42 + 42	☐ = 35 + 35	12 + 12 = ☐

Try this

Help the frog jump across the lily
pads to the fly.

The frog must jump onto a pad
with a number that is double the
number on the pad he is sitting on.

The frog must jump onto a lily
pad next to, or diagonal to, the pad
he is sitting on.

1	5	10	20	25
3	2	6	12	24
2	4	8	13	20
4	22	22	16	88
8	44	44	40	32

Learn

Each penguin eats 2 fish.
How many fish will the zookeeper
need if there are 4 penguins?

$2 \times 4 =$

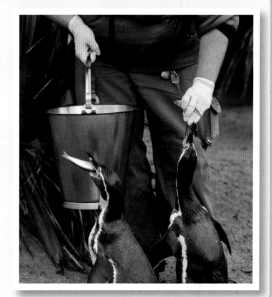

There are 8 fish.

$2 \times 4 = 8$

Practise

1 Each penguin eats 2 fish.

Use the arrays to work out how many fish the zookeeper will need
if there are …

a	5 penguins		$2 \times 5 = \square$
b	6 penguins		$2 \times 6 = \square$
c	7 penguins		$2 \times 7 = \square$
d	8 penguins		$2 \times 8 = \square$
e	9 penguins		$2 \times 9 = \square$
f	10 penguins		$2 \times 10 = \square$

2 Each iguana eats 2 mangoes.

Write a multiplication fact. Show how many mangoes the zookeeper needs if there are …

a	3 iguanas		☐ × ☐ = ☐
b	4 iguanas		☐ × ☐ = ☐
c	5 iguanas		☐ × ☐ = ☐
d	6 iguanas		☐ × ☐ = ☐
e	7 iguanas		☐ × ☐ = ☐

3 Each monkey eats 5 bananas.

Draw an array and write a matching multiplication sentence.

Show how many bananas the zookeeper needs if there are …

a	2 monkeys		☐ × ☐ = ☐
b	3 monkeys		☐ × ☐ = ☐
c	4 monkeys		☐ × ☐ = ☐
d	5 monkeys		☐ × ☐ = ☐
e	6 monkeys		☐ × ☐ = ☐

4 Explain what the array shows.

8c Division

Explore

There are 4 owlets. They eat 4 worms each.
How many worms must the owl collect?

Grouping

Learn

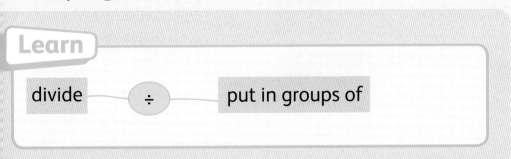

divide — ÷ — put in groups of

Key words

group
divide
equal
remainder

The baker has a packet of 21 cherries.
She puts 3 cherries on top of each cake.
How many cakes does she decorate?

21 ÷ 3 = ☐

The baker put the cherries into groups of 3.

3   6   9   12   15   18   21

There are 7 cupcakes with 3 cherries each.
There are 7 groups of 3.
21 ÷ 3 = 7

The baker has 24 pies. She puts 3 pies on each tray.
How many trays does she need?

24 ÷ 3 = ☐

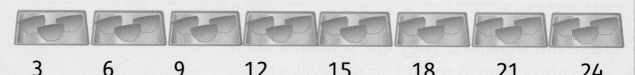

3   6   9   12   15   18   21   24

There are 8 groups of 3 pies.
The baker will need 8 trays.
24 ÷ 3 = 8

The baker put the pies into groups of 3.

Practise

1 You will need counters.

a Count 16 counters.

Put them into groups of 4.

How many groups are there?

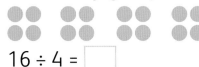

16 ÷ 4 = ☐

b Count 20 counters.

Put them into groups of 4.

How many groups are there?

20 ÷ 4 = ☐

c Count 24 counters.

Put them into groups of 4.

How many groups are there?

24 ÷ 4 = ☐

2

a The baker baked 20 biscuits.
She put 5 on each plate.
How many plates did she use?

20 ÷ 5 = ☐

b The baker baked 25 biscuits.
He put 5 on each plate.
How many plates did he use?

25 ÷ 5 = ☐

Some left over

Learn

$16 \div 5 = \boxed{}$

Put 16 counters into groups of 5.

How many groups are there?

There are 3 groups and 1 left over.

When there are some left over, we call this the remainder.

$16 \div 5 = 3$ remainder 1

The farmer has 17 eggs.

He packs them in boxes of 5.

How many boxes of 5 are there?

There are 3 groups of 5 eggs
and 2 left over.

$17 \div 5 = 3$ remainder 2

The farmer will fill 3 boxes.

The shopkeeper has 25 apples.
She packs them in bags of 6.
How many bags of 6 are there?
There are 4 groups of 6 and
1 left over.
$25 \div 6 = 4$ remainder 1
The shopkeeper will fill 4 bags.

Practise

1 You will need counters.

a Count 22 counters.
Put them into groups of 3.

How many groups are there?

22 ÷ 3 = ☐ remainder ☐

b Count 31 counters.
Put them into groups of 5.

How many groups are there?

31 ÷ 5 = ☐

c Count 30 counters.
Put them into groups of 4.

How many groups are there?

30 ÷ 4 = ☐

d Count 17 counters.
Put them into groups of 3.

How many groups are there?

17 ÷ 3 = ☐

2 The teacher had 27 pencils. She put them in groups of 4.
How many groups are there? How many pencils are left over?

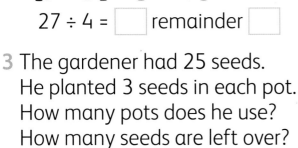

27 ÷ 4 = ☐ remainder ☐

3 The gardener had 25 seeds.
He planted 3 seeds in each pot.
How many pots does he use?
How many seeds are left over?

Try this

30 ÷ 5 = 6	6 × 5 = 30
25 ÷ 5 = 5	5 × 5 = ☐
20 ÷ 5 = 4	4 × 5 = ☐
15 ÷ 5 = 3	3 × 5 = ☐

Self-check

A Addition and subtraction

1 Copy these calculations. Write the answers.

a 10 + 53 = ☐   20 + 53 = ☐   30 + 53 = ☐

b 84 – 10 = ☐   84 – 20 = ☐   84 – 30 = ☐

c 67 – 63 = ☐   57 – 53 = ☐   47 – 43 = ☐

B Multiplication

1 a Choose two two-digit numbers. Write them down.
  b Use the numbers to make a multiplication calculation.
  c Write a story to match the calculation.
  d Draw an array to match the story.

C Division

1 Tessa played a game of marbles with her friends.
  She had 36 marbles. She put them into groups of 5.

  a Write a division calculation to match the problem.
  b How many groups of marbles did she have?
  c How many marbles were left over?

Unit 9   Measure and problem solving

9a Money

Make a total of $16 with notes and coins.
In how many different ways can you do this?

Key words
dollar
cent
coins
notes
change
pay

Making different amounts

These are the coins and notes we use.

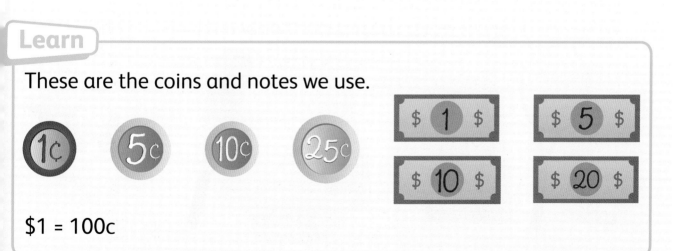

$1 = 100c

We can make any amount using these coins and notes.

$4.25 = [$ 1 $] [$ 1 $] [$ 1 $] [$ 1 $] (25¢) or

[$ 1 $] [$ 1 $] [$ 1 $] [$ 1 $] (10¢) (10¢) (5¢)

$5.30 = [$ 5 $] (10¢) (10¢) (10¢) or

[$ 1 $] [$ 1 $] [$ 1 $] [$ 1 $] [$ 1 $] (10¢) (10¢) (10¢)

Practise

1 How much money is there? The first one has been done for you.

a [$ 1 $] (10¢) **$1.10**

b [$ 1 $] [$ 1 $] [$ 1 $] (10¢)

c [$ 5 $] (25¢) (25¢)

d [$ 5 $] (25¢) (25¢) (25¢)

e [$ 5 $] [$ 1 $] (10¢) (5¢)

f [$ 5 $] [$ 5 $] (25¢) (5¢)

2 What notes and coins could you use to pay for these items?
Write two different ways. The first one has been done for you.

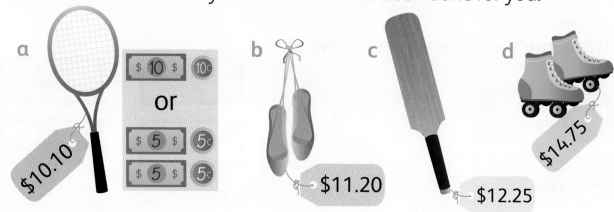

Calculating change

Sometimes when we pay for things, we need change.

Carlos buys a ball. It cost $18.
He pays with a $20 note.

$20 - $18 = ☐

These numbers are close together.
We can find the difference.
Put the smaller number in your head.
Count on. Carlos counts on 2.

$20 - $18 = $2
He needs $2 change.

10 11 12 13 14 15 16 17 18 19 20

1 Pay for the items with $20.
  How much change do you get?

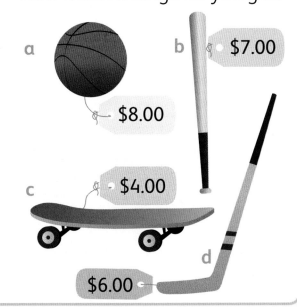

a

b $7.00

$8.00

c $4.00

d

$6.00

$7.00

$6.00

$10.00

$14.00

$4.00

Which two items could Sophia
buy with $20 so that she has
no change?

9b **Measuring mass**

Explore

Key words
weight
mass
heavier
lighter
kilograms
grams
scales

Rashid has $\frac{1}{2}$ a kilogram.

Rashid has 5 kg.

Rashid has 500 g.

Who is correct? Explain why.
How much will Rashid's nuts cost?

Reading scales

Learn

We measure the mass of an object in grams (g) and in kilograms (kg).

We can use weighing scales to measure how heavy an object is.

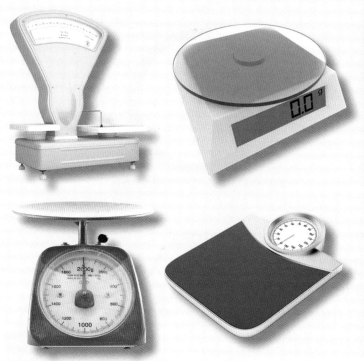

Look at the scale on the right.
What is the mass of the parcel?
The red arrow points to 80 g.
This scale measures in grams.
So the parcel weighs 80 grams.
We can record this as 80 g.

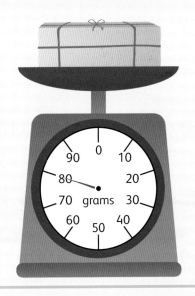

Practise

1 Write the mass of each parcel.

a

b

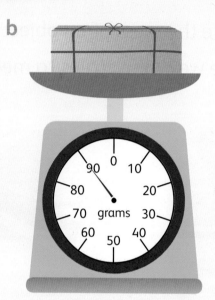

2 The children picked and then weighed tomatoes.
Rosi's tomato weighed 65 g.
Mia's tomato weighed 10 g less than Rosi's.
Julio's tomato weighed 20 g more than Mia's.
How much did Julio's tomato weigh?

Comparing the mass of objects

Learn

We can use signs to compare. | < 'is less than' | > 'is greater than' |

50 g > 2 g   100 g > 10 g   4 g < 25 g   3 g < 60 g

Practise

1 Gabriel has weighed these objects.

 10g   200g  300g   75g glue 50g

a Which object has the heaviest mass?

b Which object has the lightest mass?

c Write the objects in order from lightest to heaviest.

2 Copy these statements. Then complete them by filling in either < or >.

a 10 g ☐ 11 g   b 20 g ☐ 25 g

c 90 g ☐ 90 kg   d 20 kg ☐ 20 g

e 10 kg ☐ 9 kg   f 20 g ☐ 15 kg

3 Use the <, > or = signs to write statements.
The first one has been done for you.

a
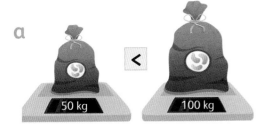

b
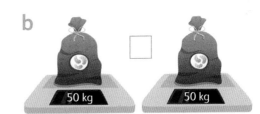

c
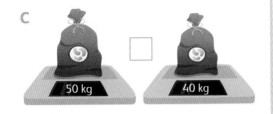

Think like a mathematician

- Mass is how heavy something is.
- Weighing scales are marked in units (grams or kilograms).

 9c **Time**

Explore

How to make a paper plate clock

You will need

- a paper plate
- a felt-tip pen
- a split pin
- a sheet of coloured card
- a pair of scissors

Method

1 Write the numbers 1 to 12 around the paper plate. Space them evenly like on a clock face.

2 Draw and cut out an hour hand and a minute hand from the coloured card.

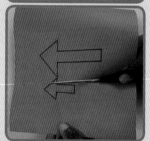

3 Use the split pin to attach the minute and hour hands to the paper plate.

4 Check that the hands can move easily. Choose a time and set the hands of the clock to show this time.

Key words

time
year
month
week
hour
minute
second
half an hour

Digital and analogue clocks

Learn

1 day = 24 hours $\frac{1}{2}$ an hour = 30 minutes
1 hour = 60 minutes   1 minute = 60 seconds

The time on an analogue clock	The time on a digital clock
	 hour minutes
What time is it? The hour hand is pointing to the 7. The minute hand is pointing to the 12. It is 7 o'clock.	It is 7 o'clock.
	 hour minutes
What time is it? The hour hand is pointing past the 9. The minute hand is pointing to the 6. It is half past 9.	It is half past 9.

Practise

1 What time is it? The first one has been done for you.

a    b   c    d

2 o'clock

2 What time is it? The first one has been done for you.

a    b    c    d

half past 2

3 Match the digital times to the analogue times. Write down the matching pairs of letters. The first one has been done for you.

a   a and h   e

b   f

c   g

d   h

Measuring time

Learn

We can measure how long activities take in minutes and seconds.
Remember: 1 minute = 60 seconds

Victor ran around the playground. The stop watch shows how long he took.

minutes   seconds

The stop watch shows 4 minutes and 30 seconds.

Practise

1 The children timed each other running around the field. How many minutes and seconds did it take them?

a
2:10

b
2:20

c
2:40

2 Work with a partner. Time how long it takes you to:
  a Pour out a bag of rice or sand.
  b Count to 100.
  c Write your name twenty times.

Try this

How long can you go without blinking? Work with a partner to time each other.

Think like a mathematician

- Half an hour = half of 60 minutes
                = 30 minutes
- Half a minute = half of 60 seconds
                = 30 seconds

Self-check

A Money

1 Lola bought a football for $8.25. What different coins or notes could she use to pay?
Draw the notes and coins. Then write the calculation.

2 Alec bought a baseball glove for $12. He paid with a $20 note. How much change did he get?

B Measuring mass

1 Write down the mass of the parcel.

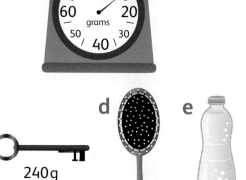

2 Put the objects in order from lightest to heaviest. Write down the order of the letters.

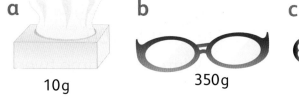

a 10g

b 350g

c 240g

d 75g

e 500g

C Measuring time

1 Write down the time on the clocks.

a

b
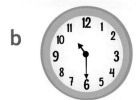

2 The stop watch shows how long Tessa balanced on one leg. For how long did she balance?

3:20

ⓘ 10a The circus

Problem 1

Look at this circus scene.

What are the differences between these two pictures?

Problem 2

The clown is making his hat.
He wants 3 pom-poms on it.

The pom-poms are red, blue and yellow.
What order could they be in?
Write the different combinations.
How many combinations are there?

Problem 3

The trapeze artist is playing a game.
She throws 3 hoops over the posts.

Each post has a different score.

The striped post scores 3 points.
The yellow post scores 2 points.
The red post scores 5 points.

What could her total score be?
Write all the possible combinations.

 3 points   2 points   5 points

Problem 4

The stilts are 86 cm high. The clown cuts 5 cm off.

How tall are the stilts now?

Problem 5

The girl cycled around the field on her unicycle. She took 86 seconds.

Her friend cycled around the field on the unicycle. He was 4 seconds faster.

How long did he take to cycle around the field?

Problem 6

The plate spinners practised spinning with 86 plates.

They broke 3 plates.

How many plates were left?

Problem 7

This table shows the number of tickets sold at the circus.

Day of the week	Number of tickets sold
Thursday	20
Friday	30
Saturday	40
Sunday	50

On which day were the most tickets sold?

On which day were the fewest tickets sold?

How many people came to the circus on Thursday and Friday altogether?

How many people came to the circus on Thursday and Saturday altogether?

How many people came to the circus on Thursday and Sunday altogether?

Problem 8

$1 $2

$2 $4

Kadir has $5.

Which 2 ice creams or lollies could he buy?

Sara has $5.

Which 3 ice creams or lollies could she buy?

Problem 9

There are 30 people in the audience.
The clown squirts water at the people.

The clown squirts 28 people.
How many people did he not squirt?

Ten people leave. How many people are
left in the audience?

Problem 10

Clown A juggles balls for 10 minutes.

Clown B juggles balls for 4 minutes less than Clown A.

Clown C juggles balls for 2 minutes longer than Clown B.

For how long does Clown C juggle?

Clown A   Clown B   Clown C

Unit 11 Number and problem solving

11a Place value and partitioning

Key words
compare
digit
tens
ones
more than
less than

Explore

How tall is Carlos' plant?

What is the nearest multiple of ten?

Rounding numbers

Learn

We can round numbers up or down to the nearest multiple of 10.
Look at the number on a number line to find its closest multiple of ten.

20 21 22 23 24 25 26 27 28 29 30

Is carriage 24 nearest to 20 or 30?

Is carriage 27 nearest to 20 or 30?

Practise

1 Round these numbers to the nearest multiple of 10.

| 43 | 58 | 29 | 31 | 81 | 35 | 76 | 92 |

More or less

Learn

To partition numbers, work out how many tens and how many ones.

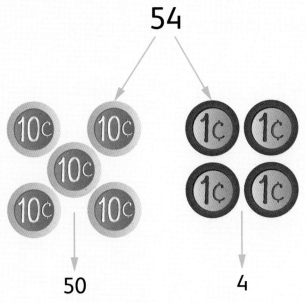

50   4

5 tens and 4 ones.

We can show partitioning like this.

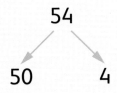

We can use partitioning to help us find 1 more, 1 less, 10 more and 10 less.

To find 1 more than 14, we add 1.

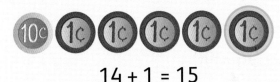

14 + 1 = 15

To find 1 less than 14, we subtract 1.

14 − 1 = 13

To find 10 more than 14, we add 10.

14 + 10 = 24

To find 10 less than 14, we subtract 10.

14 − 10 = 4

Practise

1 Partition these numbers. The first one has been done for you.

a 34 → 30, 4

b 87 → 80, ☐

c 26 → 20, ☐

d 19 → 10, ☐

2 Partition these numbers. The first one has been done for you.

a $36 = 30 + 6$

b $11 = 10 + \square$

c $43 = \square + 3$

d $66 = 60 + \square$

e $27 = \square + 7$

f $58 = \square + 8$

g $94 = 90 + \square$

h $71 = \square + 1$

3 Find 1 more, 1 less, 10 more and 10 less.
The first one has been done for you.

$94 + 1 = 95$	$19 - 1 = \square$	$31 + 10 = \square$	$55 - 10 = \square$
$95 + 1 = \square$	$18 - 1 = \square$	$32 + 10 = \square$	$56 - 10 = \square$
$98 + 1 = \square$	$12 - 1 = \square$	$14 + 10 = \square$	$65 - 10 = \square$
$88 + 1 = \square$	$22 - 1 = \square$	$24 + 10 = \square$	$75 - 10 = \square$
$78 + 1 = \square$	$32 - 1 = \square$	$34 + 10 = \square$	$85 - 10 = \square$

Try this

Write the answers to these calculations.

$29 + 1 = \square$ $11 - 1 = \square$ $92 + 10 = \square$ $12 - 10 = \square$

$39 + 1 = \square$ $21 - 1 = \square$ $93 + 10 = \square$ $13 - 10 = \square$

Ordering and comparing numbers

Learn

Ordering

24 cm   12 cm   42 cm   8 cm   17 cm

Order the bears from smallest to biggest.

42 cm

24 cm

17 cm

12 cm

8 cm

Comparing

42 cm   >   12 cm

42 cm is greater than 12 cm.

Practise

1 Order each set of numbers from smallest to biggest.

94, 83, 67, 72, 51	27, 13, 86, 56, 63
18, 46, 39, 15, 27	83, 71, 59, 64, 41
28, 31, 48, 25, 67	71, 63, 49, 58, 31

2 Copy the number sentences.
Use < or > to compare the numbers.

Remember
< means 'is less than', > means 'is greater than'.

The first one has been done for you.

a 24 < 74   b 52 ☐ 57   c 32 ☐ 23

d 63 ☐ 33   e 13 ☐ 18   f 81 ☐ 18

g 85 ☐ 95   h 73 ☐ 33   i 75 ☐ 57

Try this

Copy the number sentences.
Use the < or > signs to complete them.

a 10 cm ☐ 20 cm   b 53 g ☐ 50 g

c 14 litres ☐ 64 litres

117

11b Halves and quarters

Explore

What fraction of the children are sitting by the pool?
What other fractions can you see in the picture?

Key words
fraction
equivalent
halves
half
quarters

Equivalent fractions

What fraction is blue?

$\frac{1}{2}$ $\frac{1}{4}$ $\frac{3}{4}$

one half   one quarter   three quarters

Which fractions are the same?

1     $\frac{2}{2} = 1$ $\frac{4}{4} = 1$

$\frac{1}{2}$ $\frac{2}{4}$

1 What fraction is purple?

a   b   c

2 What fractions are the same?

1 What fraction of each shape is green? Use these fractions.

$\frac{1}{2}$ $\frac{1}{4}$ $\frac{3}{4}$

a   b

c   d

2 What fraction of each shape is NOT green?

a   b

c   d

Fractions of amounts

Learn

Find $\frac{1}{2}$ of 8.

Put them into 2 equal groups.
How many counters are there in one group?

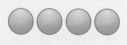 

$\frac{1}{2}$ of 8 = 4

Find $\frac{1}{4}$ of 8.

Put them into 4 equal groups.
How many counters are there in one group?

$\frac{1}{4}$ of 8 = 2

Practise

1 Find $\frac{1}{2}$ of 6. ●●●●●●

2 Use counters to find these fractions.

$\frac{1}{2}$ of 2 = ☐ $\frac{1}{2}$ of 6 = ☐

$\frac{1}{2}$ of 10 = ☐ $\frac{1}{2}$ of 14 = ☐

$\frac{1}{2}$ of 18 = ☐ $\frac{1}{2}$ of 22 = ☐

3 Use pebbles or shells to find these fractions.

$\frac{1}{4}$ of 4 = ☐ $\frac{1}{4}$ of ☐ = 3

$\frac{1}{4}$ of 16 = ☐ $\frac{1}{4}$ of 20 = ☐

$\frac{1}{4}$ of ☐ = 2 $\frac{1}{4}$ of ☐ = 10

Think like a mathematician

Remember all the parts must be e~~qual~~
Half = 2 equal groups
Quarters = 4 equal groups

Try this

Which shapes are divided into halves?

a  b   c  d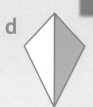

⟳ 11c Number patterns

Explore

How many animals are there altogether?

Count in twos and fours:

● How many eyes are there around the waterhole?
● How many hooves are there around the waterhole?

Counting in groups

Learn

Count in twos.

2 4 6 8 10 12 14 16 18 20

There are 20 counters.
These are all even numbers.

Count in fives.

5 10 15 20 25 30 35 40 45 50

There are 50 counters.

Count in tens.

10 20 30 40 50 60 70 80 90 100

There are 100 blocks.

We can count groups of objects in 5s.

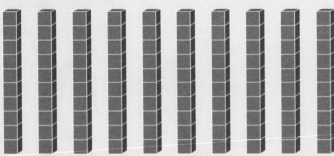

5   10   15   20   25

We can use a tally to record counting in 5s.
Each mark represents a shell. We draw the fifth mark diagonally through the previous 4 marks.
This makes the marks quicker and easier to count. ⵏⵏⵏ

Practise

1 Count the coins in each picture. Write how much money there is.
The first one has been done for you.

a 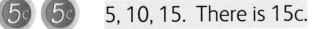 5, 10, 15. There is 15c.

b

c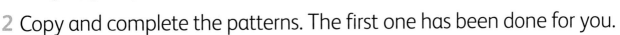

d

2 Copy and complete the patterns. The first one has been done for you.

a 0, 2, 4, 6, 8, 10   b 0, 5, 10, ____, ____, ____

c ____, 4, ____, 8, 10, ____   d ____, 30, ____, 40, 45, ____

3 Copy and complete the patterns.

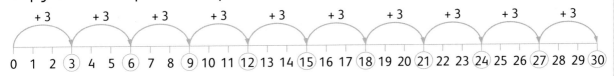

a 0, 3, 6, ____, ____, ____   b 0, ____, 6, 9, ____, ____

c 15, 18, 21, ____, ____, ____   d ____, 18, ____, 24, 27, ____

4 Copy and complete the patterns.

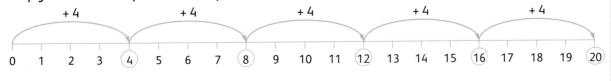

a 0, 4, 8, ____, ____, ____   b 0, ____, 8, 12, ____, ____

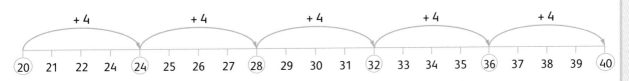

c 20, 24, 28, ____, ____, ____   d ____, 24, ____, 32, 36, ____

Multiples of 2, 5 and 10

Learn

All multiples of 2 are even numbers.
2, 4, 6, 8, 10, 12, 14, 16, 18, 20

All multiples of 5 end in the digit 5 or 0.
5, 10, 15, 20, 25, 30, 35, 40, 45, 50

All multiples of 10 end in the digit 0.
10, 20, 30, 40, 50, 60, 70, 80, 90, 100

Practise

1 Macie is playing a game. She rolls a ball to knock over the bottles. She knocks down the bottles with multiples of 2 on them. Which bottles did she knock down?

2 Julio is watching a hockey match. At the end of the match, a player on the winning team is wearing a number that is a multiple of 5.
Which is the winning team?

3 Write down all the numbers that are a multiple of 10.

12   20   10   38   35

17   30   71   70

Try this

Complete the Venn diagram.

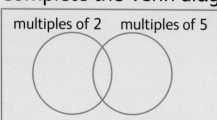

1, 2, 5, 4, 10, 6, 15, 20, 8, 12, 25, 30, 14, 19

Self-check

A Place value and partitioning

1 Partition these numbers.

  a 26   b 53   c 74

2 Amelie has 12 apples in her basket. She picks 10 more apples. How many apples are there?

3 Copy and complete the number sentences.

  23 > ☐   76 < ☐   82 = ☐

B Halves and quarters

1 Alec had $6. He spent half. How much money did Alec spend?

2 Which shapes have $\frac{1}{2}$ shaded? Write the letters.

a 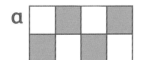 b 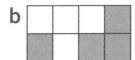 c 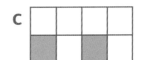 d

C Number patterns

1 Each flower has 5 petals. How many petals are there?

Count in fives. Draw a number line to help you.

2 At a birthday party, the balloons are tied in groups of 3. There are 4 bunches. How many balloons are there?

3 Look at this Venn diagram. Write the headings for boxes a and b.

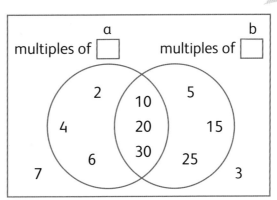

12a 2-D and 3-D shapes

Explore

Key words

circle
triangle
square
rectangle
pentagon
hexagon
octagon
2-D
3-D
symmetrical
faces
vertices
edges

How many squares can you see?

What shape are the dominoes?

Is the board symmetrical?

Features of shapes

2-D shapes

Object	Name of shape	Description/features
	circle	0 corners 1 curved side
	triangle	3 corners 3 sides
	square	4 square corners 4 sides of equal length
	rectangle	4 square corners 4 sides Opposite sides are equal length.
	hexagon	6 corners 6 sides

3-D shapes

Object	Name of shape	Description/features
	cone	1 corner, 1 face, 1 curved surface
	cuboid	8 corners, 6 faces, 12 edges
	sphere	1 curved surface
	cylinder	2 faces, 1 curved surface

Practise

1 Write two special features of each shape. The first one has been done for you.

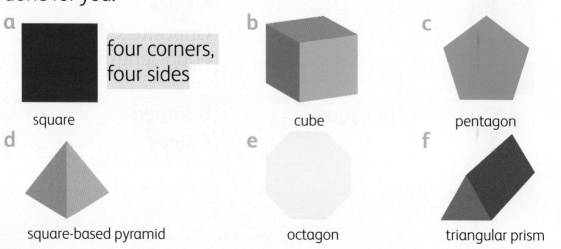

a four corners, four sides
square

b
cube

c
pentagon

d
square-based pyramid

e
octagon

f
triangular prism

2 Sort each set of shapes into two groups. Explain your groups.

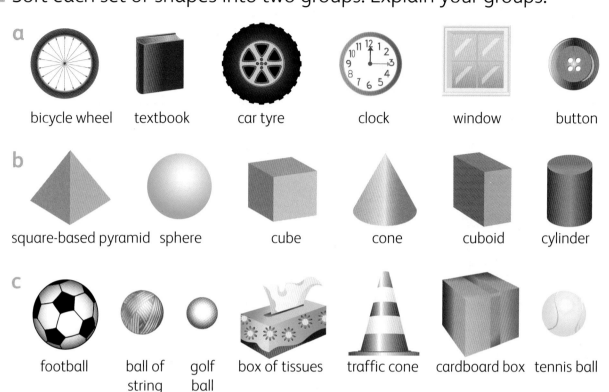

a

bicycle wheel   textbook   car tyre   clock   window   button

b

square-based pyramid   sphere   cube   cone   cuboid   cylinder

c

football   ball of string   golf ball   box of tissues   traffic cone   cardboard box   tennis ball

Symmetry

Learn

A line of symmetry shows where we can fold a shape in half symmetrically.

A symmetrical shape is the same on both sides of a line of symmetry.

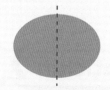

line of symmetry   line of symmetry   line of symmetry   line of symmetry   line of symmetry

Practise

1 Which lines of symmetry are correct?
Write the letters of the correct shapes.

a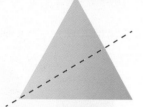

b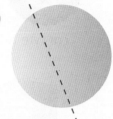

c

d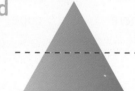

2 Which shapes have a line of symmetry? Copy and complete the table.

3 Use 10 cubes. Make a symmetrical shape.

Draw a picture of it.

Shape		✗ or ✓	Shape		✗ or ✓
a	▲		d	⬠	
b	▰		e	⬠	
c	◺		f	▭	

Think like a mathematician

You can use a mirror to check if a shape or pattern is symmetrical.

12b Position and movement

Where is the parrot?

Key words

direction
position
forwards
backwards
left
right
anti-clockwise
clockwise
whole-turn
half-turn
quarter-turn
rotate
turn

Position and movement

Learn

You use directions when you tell someone how to get somewhere.

turn left	turn right	forwards	backwards

Practise

This is how to get to the school.
Step one square forwards. Step one square left. Go forwards three squares. Move right one square. You have arrived at school.

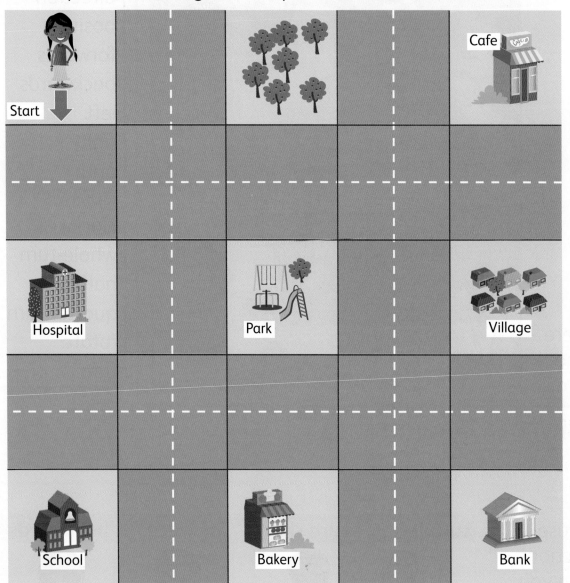

1 Use the map. Write directions from Start to …

   a the hospital   b the park   c the bakery

   d the village   e the school   f the bank.

2 Start in square 2B each time. Follow the directions.
Which square does the tiger walk to?

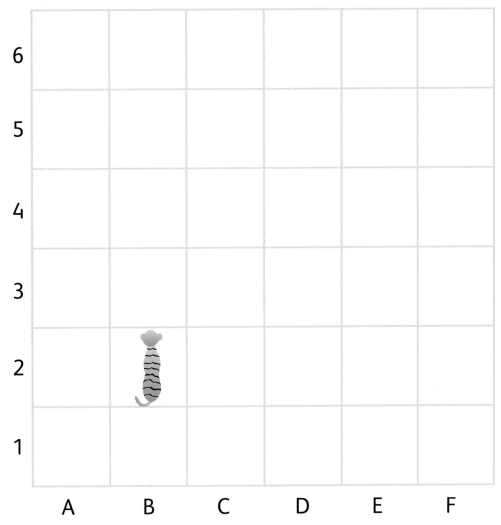

a 2 squares forwards, turn right, 1 square forwards.

b 1 square backwards, turn right, 3 squares forwards.

c 1 square left, 4 squares forwards.

d 3 squares forwards, turn right, 1 square backwards.

e 3 squares forwards, turn right, 2 squares backwards.

f 1 square forwards, turn right, 3 squares forwards.

Try this

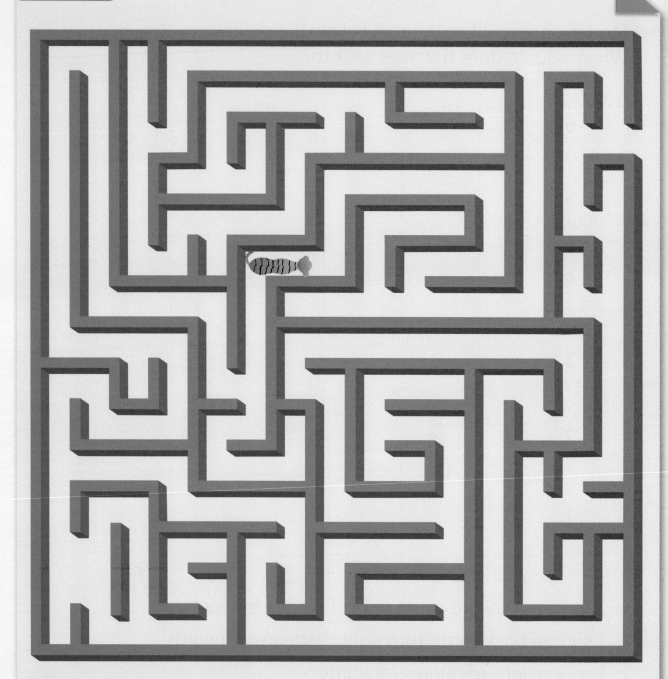

The tiger is lost. Help him find his way out of the maze.

Write the directions.

Whole, half- and quarter-turns

Learn

A turn changes the direction you are facing. Your position stays the same.

You can turn in different ways.

Clockwise	Anticlockwise

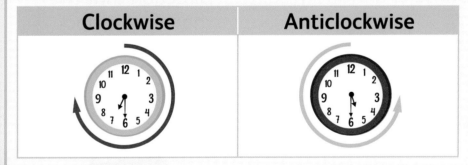

You can turn in different amounts.

Whole-turn	Half-turn	Quarter-turn

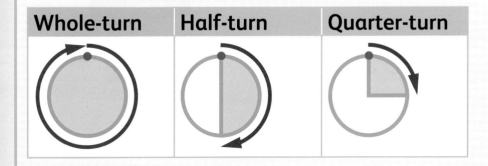

A quarter-turn is the same as a right angle.

A quarter-turn, clockwise

You can turn shapes and objects.

Practise

1 Look at the shape.

Garon turns the shape a quarter-turn.

Did he turn it clockwise or anticlockwise?

a   b

2 Look at the shape.

Rosi turns it clockwise.

Did she turn it a half-turn or a quarter-turn?

a   b

Think of the direction that the hands of a clock move. They move in a clockwise direction.

3 Look at the shape.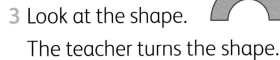
The teacher turns the shape.

He turned it
quarter of a turn.

He turned it
half of a turn.

Who is correct?

Try this

Which shapes have right angles?

a

b
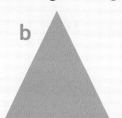

c

d

Think like a Mathematician

- A whole turn is four right angles
  or a full rotation.
- A half-turn is two right angles.
- A quarter-turn is one right angle.

137

Self-check

A 2-D and 3-D shapes

1 Look at the picture.

   a Write the names of the 2-D shapes you can see in the picture.

   b Copy and complete the tables about the shapes in the picture.

2-D shapes	Number of sides

Shapes with 4 sides	Shapes not with 4 sides

B Position and movement

1 Write directions to move the bee to:

   a C3   b D1   c A5.

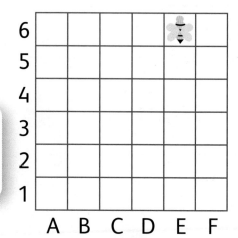

Start with the bee in E6 each time.

2 Draw the bee after the turn.

   a A quarter-turn clockwise

   b A half-turn anticlockwise

13a Addition and subtraction

Explore

Tamika made a shell necklace.
She used the pink shells and the blue shells.
How many shells did she use?

Key words

addition
subtraction
find the difference
two-digit numbers
tens
ones
multiple

Addition

Learn

35 + 24 =

Partition the numbers into tens and ones.

35

24

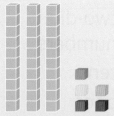

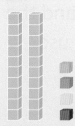

There are 3 tens and 5 ones.   There are 2 tens and 4 ones.

Add the tens.
3 tens + 2 tens = 5 tens
30 + 20 = 50

Add the ones.
5 ones + 4 ones = 9 ones
5 + 4 = 9

Add these together.
50 + 9 = 59

The answer is 59.

35 + 24 = 59

Practise

1 Write the answers. The first one has been done for you.

1 + 2 = 3	☐ = 10 + 20	3 + 1 = ☐	☐ = 30 + 10
1 + 3 = ☐	☐ = 10 + 30	3 + 2 = ☐	☐ = 30 + 20
1 + 4 = ☐	☐ = 10 + 40	3 + 3 = ☐	☐ = 30 + 30

2 Write the totals. The first one has been done for you.

20 + 1 = 21	☐ = 30 + 4	40 + 7 = ☐	☐ = 50 + 1
20 + 2 = ☐	☐ = 30 + 5	40 + 8 = ☐	☐ = 50 + 2
20 + 3 = ☐	☐ = 30 + 6	40 + 9 = ☐	☐ = 50 + 3

3 Work these out. The first one has been done for you.

53 + 1 = 54	☐ = 21 + 5	72 + 1 = ☐	☐ = 42 + 3
53 + 2 = ☐	☐ = 21 + 6	72 + 2 = ☐	☐ = 42 + 4
53 + 3 = ☐	☐ = 21 + 7	72 + 3 = ☐	☐ = 42 + 5

4 Write the totals. The first one has been done for you.

1 + 2 = 3	☐ = 3 + 4	5 + 2 = ☐	☐ = 6 + 1
10 + 20 = ☐	☐ = 30 + 40	50 + 20 = ☐	☐ = 60 + 10
10 + 21 = ☐	☐ = 30 + 42	50 + 27 = ☐	☐ = 60 + 13
11 + 21 = ☐	☐ = 34 + 42	52 + 27 = ☐	☐ = 62 + 13

Try this

The stall holder buys 23 oranges and 45 passion fruit from the farmer.

How many pieces of fruit does she have altogether?

Subtraction

Learn

Counting back

To work out 27 − 3 = ☐
we can **count back**.
Remember the bigger number.

Count back the smaller number.
The answer is 24.

Use a number line.

27 − 3 = ☐

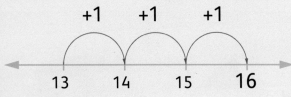

Counting on

If the numbers are close
together, we **count on** to find
the difference.

16 − 13 = ☐

Start at the smaller number and
count on to the bigger number.

The answer is 3.

Counting back across the tens

43 − 7 = ☐

Count back to the multiple
of ten first.

Then take away 4 more.

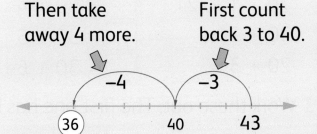

43 − 7 = 36

Counting on across the tens

33 − 28 = ☐

Count on to the multiple
of ten first.

Then count on to the bigger
number.

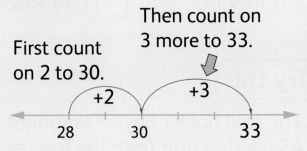

3 + 2 = 5
So 33 − 28 = 5

Practise

1 Take away to work out the answers.

43 − 7 = ☐   52 − 4 = ☐   26 − 8 = ☐   23 − 5 = ☐

62 − 5 = ☐   33 − 6 = ☐   32 − 7 = ☐   85 − 7 = ☐

2 Find the difference.

32 − 27 = ☐   43 − 38 = ☐   74 − 69 = ☐   81 − 76 = ☐

53 − 47 = ☐   34 − 29 = ☐   62 − 57 = ☐   92 − 88 = ☐

3 Solve the word problems.

a There were 43 people on the bus. At the first stop, 6 people climbed off. How many people were left on the bus?

b At the cake stall there were 43 cakes. 37 cakes were sold. How many cakes were left?

Try this

1 Maria collected 23 shells on the beach. Five were broken. How many whole shells did Maria have?

2 Carlos counted 24 sail boats at sea. 19 had their sails up. How many boats did not have their sails up?

Explain how you solved the problems.

Think like a mathematician

Count back across the tens: 52 − 7 = 45

Then take away 5 more.   Count back to the multiple of 10 first.

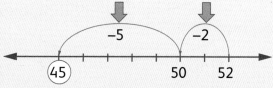

Count on across the tens: 43 − 38 = 5

Count on to the multiple of 10 first.   Then count on to the bigger number.

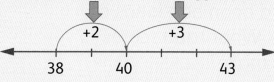

13b Multiplication and division

Explore

Akio is playing a game. He throws bean bags at the target. If a bean bag lands in the outer ring, he scores double the number.

Key words
double
times table
multiple
multiply
divide
group
share

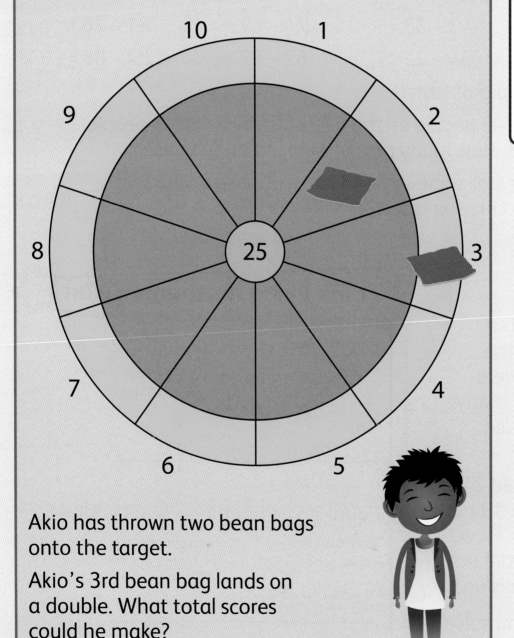

Akio has thrown two bean bags onto the target.

Akio's 3rd bean bag lands on a double. What total scores could he make?

Multiplication

Learn

2× table	3× table	4× table	5× table
2 × 1 = **2**	3 × 1 = **3**	4 × 1 = **4**	5 × 1 = **5**
2 × 2 = **4**	3 × 2 = **6**	4 × 2 = **8**	5 × 2 = **10**
2 × 3 = **6**	3 × 3 = **9**	4 × 3 = **12**	5 × 3 = **15**
2 × 4 = **8**	3 × 4 = **12**	4 × 4 = **16**	5 × 4 = **20**
2 × 5 = **10**	3 × 5 = **15**	4 × 5 = **20**	5 × 5 = **25**
2 × 6 = **12**	3 × 6 = **18**	4 × 6 = **24**	5 × 6 = **30**
2 × 7 = **14**	3 × 7 = **21**	4 × 7 = **28**	5 × 7 = **35**
2 × 8 = **16**	3 × 8 = **24**	4 × 8 = **32**	5 × 8 = **40**
2 × 9 = **18**	3 × 9 = **27**	4 × 9 = **36**	5 × 9 = **45**
2 × 10 = **20**	3 × 10 = **30**	4 × 10 = **40**	5 × 10 = **50**

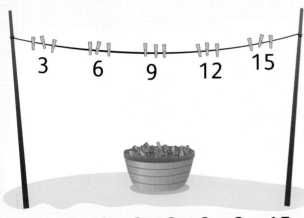

3   6   9   12   15

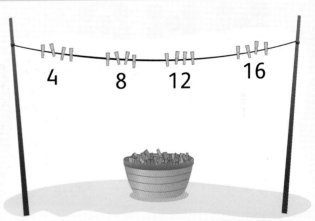

4   8   12   16

$3 \times 5 = 3 + 3 + 3 + 3 + 3 = 15$

$4 \times 4 = 4 + 4 + 4 + 4 = 16$

Practise your 2x, 3x, 4x, and 5x tables.

Practise

1 Write these doubles. The first one has been done for you.

a ⎕ + ⎕ = **2 glasses of juice**

b 👟👟 + 👟👟 = ____   c 🔘🔘 + 🔘🔘 = ____

d 🍬🍬🍬 + 🍬🍬🍬 = ____

e ●●●●● + ●●●●● = ____

2 How many counters are there in each picture?
Write a number sentence to match.

a ●● ●●   b ●●● ●●●   c ●●● ●●●
●● ●●   ●●● ●●●

d ●●● ●●● ●●●   e ●●● ●●● ●●● ●●●

3 Write these doubles. Two have been done for you.

a 6 + 6 = 12   b 15 + 15 = 30   c 12 + 12 = ⎕
7 + 7 = ⎕   20 + 20 = ⎕   24 + 24 = ⎕
8 + 8 = ⎕   25 + 25 = ⎕   34 + 34 = ⎕
9 + 9 = ⎕   50 + 50 = ⎕   36 + 36 = ⎕

4 Solve the word problems.

a Oranges were sold in bags of 14.
Gabriel bought 2 bags.
How many oranges did he have?

b Lemons were sold in bags of 16.
Maria bought 2 bags.
How many lemons did she have?

Remember that
double means
'two lots of'
a number.

Copy and complete the Venn diagram. Sort the multiples of 3 and 4.

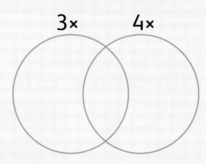

3	4	32	10
18	15	20	12
30	40	36	16
21	24	28	27
6	8	9	5

Division

$12 ÷ 4 = \boxed{}$

Sofia had 12 counters.
She put them into groups of 4.
How many groups of 4 make 12?

Division facts: ÷ 5	
5 ÷ 5 = 1	30 ÷ 5 = 6
10 ÷ 5 = 2	35 ÷ 5 = 7
15 ÷ 5 = 3	40 ÷ 5 = 8
20 ÷ 5 = 4	45 ÷ 5 = 9
25 ÷ 5 = 5	50 ÷ 5 = 10

There are 3 groups.
The answer is 3.
$12 ÷ 4 = 3$

$13 ÷ 4 = \boxed{}$

Amelie had 13 counters.
She put them into groups of 4.
How many groups of 4 make 13?

Learn these fun division facts!

● 1 left over

There are 3 groups and 1 left over.
$13 ÷ 4 = 3$ remainder 1

Division facts: ÷ 10	
10 ÷ 10 = 1	60 ÷ 10 = 6
20 ÷ 10 = 2	70 ÷ 10 = 7
30 ÷ 10 = 3	80 ÷ 10 = 8
40 ÷ 10 = 4	90 ÷ 10 = 9
50 ÷ 10 = 5	100 ÷ 10 = 10

Practise

1 Copy and complete these. Put counters into groups to find how many groups there are. The first one has been done for you.

$10 \div 5 = \boxed{2}$	$12 \div 4 = \square$	$15 \div 3 = \square$	$30 \div 10 = \square$
$15 \div 5 = \square$	$16 \div 4 = \square$	$18 \div 3 = \square$	$40 \div 10 = \square$
$20 \div 5 = \square$	$20 \div 4 = \square$	$21 \div 3 = \square$	$50 \div 10 = \square$
$25 \div 5 = \square$	$24 \div 4 = \square$	$24 \div 3 = \square$	$60 \div 10 = \square$

What do you notice? Can you see any multiplication facts?

2 Work out if there will be some left over. Two have been done for you.

$10 \div 5 =$ 2 none left over	$12 \div 4$	$15 \div 3$
$11 \div 5 =$ 2 remainder 1	$13 \div 4$	$16 \div 3$
$12 \div 5$	$14 \div 4$	$17 \div 3$

3 Solve the problems.

a There were 6 children. The tennis coach put them into teams of 2. How many teams were there?

b There were 20 children. The cricket coach put them into groups of 5. How many groups were there?

c There were 18 children. The football coach put them into groups of 3. How many groups were there?

Try this

Write a word problem for this calculation:

$16 \div 4 = \square$

Think like a mathematician

Remember to use equal groups when you divide.
Sometimes there might be some left over after putting numbers and objects into groups.

13c Missing number problems

Lucas picked 20 guavas.

Some fell out.

How many guavas are left in the basket? How many guavas fell out?

Missing numbers

Learn

There are 20 counters in total. How many are under the cup?

Write a calculation to show the problem.

$14 + \triangle = 20$

The triangle shows a missing number.

We can use different symbols to show a missing number.

$14 + \square = 20$ $14 + ? = 20$

The answer is 6.

$14 + \mathbf{6} = 20$

We can show the addition calculation using tens frames.

Unit 13 Number and problem solving

Practise

1 What are the missing numbers? Use counters to help.

a
10 = ? + 6	4 = 10 − ?	20 = ☐ + 6	20 = ☐ + 6
10 = 5 + ?	? = 10 − 5	20 = 15 + ☐	20 = 15 + ☐
? + 4 = 10	10 − ? = 6	☐ + 4 = 20	☐ + 4 = 20
7 + ? = 10	10 − 3 = ?	17 + ☐ = 20	17 + ☐ = 20

b
30 = △ + 1	90 − △ = 20
32 = △ + 3	80 − △ = 30
34 = △ + 5	70 − △ = 40
36 = △ + 7	60 − △ = 50

What do you notice about the calculations?

2 Solve these word problems. Write the number sentence and the answer. The first one has been done for you.

   a The monkey had 10 bananas. She ate some. There were 8 left. How many did she eat? 10 − ? = 8. She ate 2 bananas.

   b The penguin had 20 fish. He ate some. There were 18 left. How many did he eat?

   c The elephant had 30 mangoes. She ate some. There were 28 left. How many did she eat?

3 Write your own problem to match each calculation.

   a 10 − ? = 9   b 20 − △ = 19   c ☐ − 1 = 29

Try this

Check these subtractions by doing an addition.

a 10 − ? = 2

b 12 = 20 − △

c 30 − ☐ = 22

Think like a mathematician

Check your addition calculations by adding again in a different order. Check your subtraction calculations by adding.

Self-check

A Addition and subtraction

1 On Saturday the baker baked 36 loaves of bread. She sold 32. How many loaves were left?

2 On Monday the baker baked 18 loaves of bread. She sold 6. How many loaves were left?

3 On Wednesday the baker baked 27 loaves of bread. At the end of the day there were 4 left. How many loaves did the baker sell that day?

Check if the numbers are close together. Choose which numbers to use to solve the problem.

B Multiplication and division
Calculate the answers.

1 $3 + 3 = \square$

2 $5 + 5 + 5 = \square$

3 Count in tens to work out how much money there is. Write the number sentence and the total.

4 $12 \div 4 = \square$

5 There were 2 football teams. Each team had 8 players. How many players were there altogether?

6 There were 20 children. The teacher divided them into teams of 4. How many teams were there?

C Missing number problems

1 $23 + ? = 30$ 2 $30 - ? = 23$

Make up a story for one of the calculations.

Unit 14 Measure and problem solving

14a Money

Explore

RIDES

Helter-skelter - $3
Carousel - $4
Tea-cup ride - $5

SNACKS

Ice cream - $1.50
Bag of nuts - $2

Rashid has $10. How many rides can he go on?

Mary has $7. How many different rides can she go on?

How many rides can they go on together?

Key words
dollar
cent
coins
notes
change
pay

Money

These are the coins and notes we use.

$1 = 100c

Making different amounts

We can make any amount using these coins and notes.

$1.50 = [$ 1 $] (25¢) (25¢) or [$ 1 $] (50¢)

$2.50 = [$ 1 $] [$ 1 $] (50¢) or [$ 1 $] (50¢) (50¢) (50¢)

Calculating change

Sometimes when we pay for things, we might need change.

Rashid goes on the helter-skelter five times. It cost $15. He pays with a $20 note.

$20 – $15 = ☐

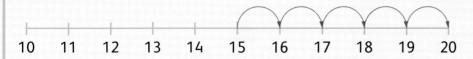

Rashid counts on 5.

$20 – $15 = $5   He needs $5 change.

Practise

1 How much money? The first one has been done for you.

a  = $2.10

b

c

d

2 What coins and notes could you use to pay for these? Write two different ways.

a $1.50

b $5.75

3 The children pay with a $20 note. How much change would they get?

a $5

Manuel had two rides on the tea-cup ride.

b $3

Jade had three rides on the helter-skelter.

Try this

How much do two ice creams cost?

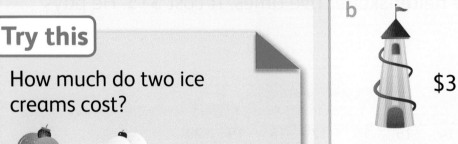

$1.50 $1.50

14b Measuring capacity

Explore

Carlito, Emilio and Renata water the plants.
They each use 4 litres of water.

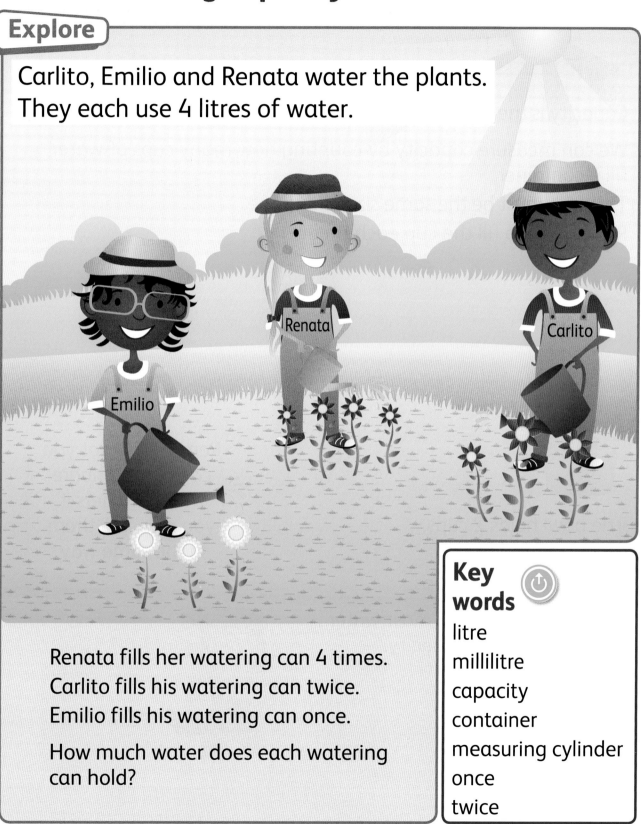

Renata fills her watering can 4 times.
Carlito fills his watering can twice.
Emilio fills his watering can once.

How much water does each watering
can hold?

Key words

litre
millilitre
capacity
container
measuring cylinder
once
twice

Estimating and comparing the capacity of containers using cups and bottles

Learn

Capacity is the amount that a container can hold.

We can measure capacity by counting how many cups of water fill a container.
The cups must be the same size and shape.
Remember to fill the cup each time.

The bowl holds 2 cups.
The jug holds 3 cups.
The bucket holds 4 cups.

The bucket holds the most water.
It has the largest capacity.

Remember that you can only compare the containers if you measure them in the same way.

Practise

You will need a selection of containers.

1 Draw and complete a table like the one below.

2 Estimate which container holds the most water.

3 How many cups of water does each container hold?

Container	Estimate	Number of cups

4 Which container holds the most water?

5 Which container holds the least water?

6 Put the containers in order from 'holds the least' to 'holds the most'.

7 a Estimate how many jam jars of water will fill the watering can.

   b Estimate how many bottles of water will fill the jug.

   c Estimate if the watering can or jug holds the most water.

watering can   jam jar   jug   water bottle

Try this

I think the measuring cylinder has the largest capacity. It is the tallest.

measuring cylinder

bottle

cup

Is Ace correct?
Explain why or why not.

Measuring in litres and millilitres

Learn

We measure capacity in litres (ℓ) and millilitres (ml).

We use the symbol ℓ for litres.
We use the symbol ml for millilitres.

We use measuring jugs and measuring cylinders to measure the capacity of containers.

The water level is at the 300 ml mark.
There is 300 ml of water in the jug.

Using the symbols makes it quick and easy to write the measurement.

Practise

1 How much water is in each measuring container?

a
ml —500
450 —
—400
350 —
—300
250 —
—200
150 —
—100
50 —

b
ml
— 500
— 450
— 400
— 350
— 300
— 250
— 200
— 150
— 100
— 50

c
ml
— 500
— 450
— 400
— 350
— 300
— 250
— 200
— 150
— 100
— 50

2 Copy the number sentences. Use <, > or = to compare the amounts.

a 100 ml ☐ 50 ml

b 100 ml ☐ 150 ml

c 3 ℓ ☐ 1 litre

d 2 ℓ ☐ 1 ℓ

e 2 ℓ ☐ 3 ℓ

f 2 ℓ ☐ 2 ℓ

3 Use <, > or = to compare the amounts.

a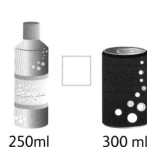

250ml   300 ml

b  ☐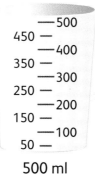

—500
450 —
—400
350 —
—300
250 —
—200
150 —
—100
50 —

250 ml   500 ml

c

300 ml   200 ml

Try this

There is 500 ml of water in the bottle.
Nina drinks 100 ml. Kobe has a drink from the bottle too.
There is 100 ml left. How much did Kobe drink?

500 ml

 **14c Time**

Explore

What is happening in July?

Key words

time
calendar
year
month
week
hour
minute
second
half an hour

JULY						
Sunday	Monday	Tuesday	Wednesday	Thursday	Friday	Saturday
						1
2	3	4	5	6 Jade's birthday	7	8 Jade's party
9	10	11	12	13	14	Gran 15 coming to stay
16	17	18 Sports day	19	20	21	22
23	24	25 Haircut	26	27 Dentist	28	29
30	31					

Digital and analogue clocks

Learn

1 day = 24 hours   1 hour = 60 minutes
$\frac{1}{2}$ hour = 30 minutes   1 minute = 60 seconds

The time on an analogue clock	The time on a digital clock
 What time is it? The hour hand is pointing to the 3. The minute hand is pointing to the 12. It is 3 o'clock.	 hour minutes It is 3 o'clock
 What time is it? The hour hand is pointing past the 3. The minute hand is pointing to the 6. It is half past 3.	 hour minutes It is half past 3.

We can measure how long activities take in minutes and seconds.
Remember 1 minute = 60 seconds.

Carlos rode his bicycle around the school.
The stop watch shows how long it took him.

The stop watch shows 3 minutes and 20 seconds.

hour   minutes

Practise

1 What time is it? The first one has been done for you.

a    b 8:00   c 10:00   d

7 o'clock

2 What time is it? The first one has been done for you.

a    b    c    d

half past 7

3 Match the digital times to the analogue times.
Write the matching sets of letters.

a

b

c

d

e

f

g

h

Try this

The aeroplane took off at 3 o'clock. I landed at 5 o'clock.

How long was the flight?

Days of the week and months of the year

Learn

Sunday Monday Tuesday Wednesday Thursday Friday Saturday

December January February March April May June July August September October November

There are 7 days in a week.
There are 24 hours in a day.
There are 60 minutes in an hour.
There are 60 seconds in a minute.   There are 12 months in a year.

Practise

1 Which day comes after Wednesday?

2 Which day comes after Friday?

3 Which day comes before Monday?

4 Which day comes before Friday?

5 Which month comes after January?

6 Which month comes before January?

7 Which month comes after June?

8 Which month comes before June?

JANUARY						
SUN	MON	TUES	WED	THU	FRI	SAT
			1	2	3	4
5	6	7	8	9	10	11
12	13	14	15	16	17	18
19	20	21	22	23	24	25
26	27	28	29	30	31	

Self-check

A Money

1 Lola bought a fish for $3.75. What different coins or notes could she use to buy it with?

2 Alec bought a teddy bear for $17. He paid with a $20 note. How much change did he get?

B Measuring capacity

1 How much water is in the measuring cylinder?

2 Copy the capacity sentences.
Fill in the <, > or = signs to compare the amounts.

a 5 litres ☐ 10 litres

b 400 ml ☐ 300 ml

c 5 litres ☐ 1 litre

ml
— 500
— 450
— 400
— 350
— 300
— 250
— 200
— 150
— 100
— 50

C Measuring time

1 What time is it?

a

b

2 Which month comes after February?

3 Which day comes before Tuesday?

15a Sports

Problem 1

This graph shows children's favourite sports.

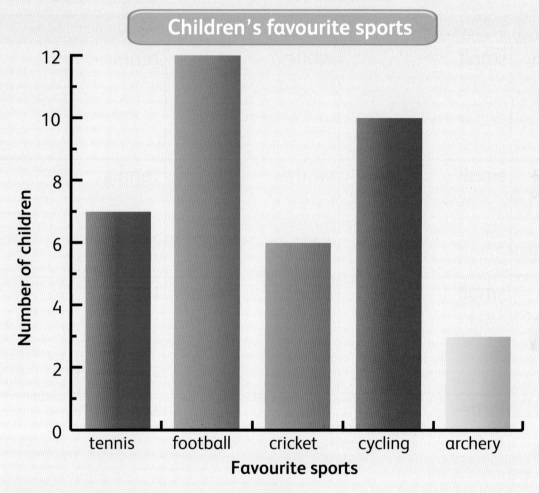

Children's favourite sports

Which is the most popular sport?

Which is the least popular sport?

How many children like cycling?

How many more children like football than cycling?

How many more children like cricket than archery?

How many children answered the questions altogether?

Problem 2

The teacher finds a tennis shoe in the lost property box.
Use the table to work out who the shoe belongs to.
The shoe is small. It is white.
It belongs to someone whose name begins with an M.

Name	Shoe size	Colour of shoes	Favourite sport
Yasmin	small	white	tennis
Maria	small	white	tennis
Kadir	small	blue	tennis
Rashid	large	blue	swimming
Sara	large	white	swimming

Who does the shoe belong to?

Problem 3

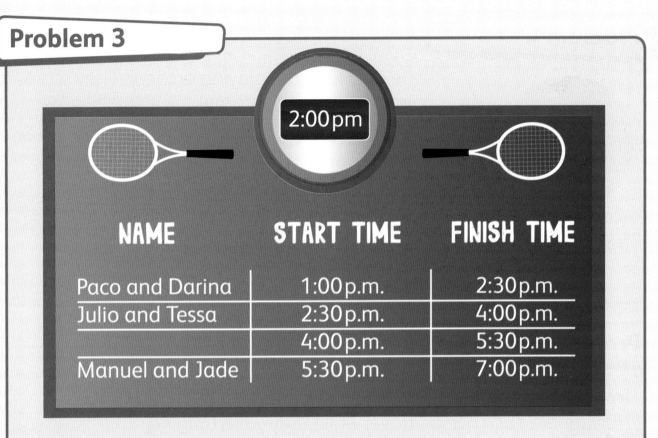

NAME	START TIME	FINISH TIME
Paco and Darina	1:00 p.m.	2:30 p.m.
Julio and Tessa	2:30 p.m.	4:00 p.m.
	4:00 p.m.	5:30 p.m.
Manuel and Jade	5:30 p.m.	7:00 p.m.

For how long will Paco and Darina play tennis?

What time will Manuel and Jade start playing tennis?

What time will Julio and Tessa finish playing tennis?

The children are discussing the time they could play tennis.

Who is correct?

What time could Kadir and Macie play tennis?

Problem 4

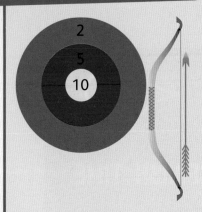

Kobe and Jade are playing archery. They score points by hitting the target.

The yellow zone scores 10 points. The red zone scores 5 points. The blue zone scores 2 points.

Jade hits the target board with 2 arrows. What could her score be?

Kobe hits the target board with 3 arrows. What could his score be?

Problem 5

In the triathlon, everyone swims, runs and cycles.
How far did each person travel while they were training?

Alec ran 3 km.
He swam 1 km.
He cycled 4 km.
How far did Alec go?

Lia ran 3 km.
She swam 1 km.
She cycled 5 km.
How far did Lia go?

Alfia ran 3 km.
She swam 1 km.
She cycled 6 km.
How far did Alfia go?

Who went the furthest in their training?

Problem 6

The children are playing cricket in teams.
They score points for the number of runs they make.

Team	Total Score
Team A	79
Team B	73
Team C	77
Team D	
Team E	69

Write the difference between team A's score and team B's score?

79 – 73 = ☐

Write the difference between team A's score and team C's score?

Write the difference between team A's score and team E's score?

Team D came second. What is their score?

The children are discussing the scores.

By how many points did Team A win?

Team A won by one or two points.

Team A won by hundreds of points.

Whose answer is reasonable?

Problem 7

The children are playing a game.
Write a story for each calculation.

2 + 3 + 4 = ☐

2 + 4 + 4 = ☐

2 + 5 + 4 = ☐

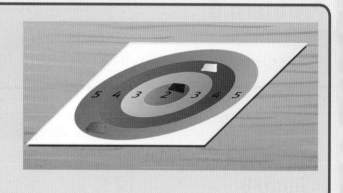

Problem 8

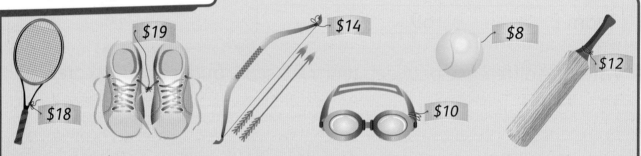

$19 $14 $8

$18 $10 $12

Victor has $20. He buys the trainers.
How much money does he have left?

Bonita has $20. She buys the tennis racket.
How much money does she have left?

Carlos has $20. He buys the bow and arrows.
How much money does he have left?

Tania has $20. What two items could she buy?

Problem 9

At a fun run there is a drink of water for
each runner during the race.

There were 87 runners.

9 drinks were left. How many runners
had a drink?

Mathematical dictionary

2-D shape a flat shape with sides and angles

3-D shape a solid shape with faces, edges and vertices

A

add to find a sum

addition a calculation of the sum of two numbers or things

anticlockwise in the opposite direction to the hands of a clock

array a rectangular arrangement of quantities

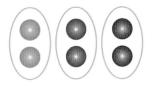

B

backwards a direction towards the back

block graph a diagram to show information

C

calculation a way of finding the number of something

capacity the largest amount that something can contain

Carroll diagram a table used for sorting things, for example:

	Multiple of 5	Not a multiple of 5
Even number	10, 20, 30	2, 6, 12
Not an even number	5, 15, 25	3, 7, 11

cent(s) a coin value

centimetre there are 100 centimetres in a metre

change money given back if you pay with too much money

circle a flat or 2-D shape with one curved surface

clockwise in the same direction as the hands of a clock

coin a piece of metal used as money

compare to note similarities and differences

container an object that holds something

corner where two or more lines meet and form an angle

corner

criterion a rule on which to base a decision

cube a 3-D or solid shape with six square faces

cuboid a 3-D or solid shape with six rectangular faces

cylinder a 3-D object or solid shape with one curved face and circular ends

D

data information, such as a tally or fact

digit symbol for a number

direction the course that something moves

divide to find how many times a number is contained in another number

dollar a unit of money

double twice as many

E

edge the straight side of a 2-D object; where two faces of a 3-D shape meet

edge

equal(s) the same as, shown by the sign =

equivalent the same as something else

estimate guess

even number all numbers ending in 0, 2, 4, 6 or 8

F

face surface of a solid shape

find the difference subtract one thing from another

face

forwards a direction towards the front

fraction a part of something or part of a number, for example $\frac{1}{2}$

G

gram there are 1000 grams in a kilogram

group to gather/collect

H

half/halves something divided by 2

half an hour 30 minutes

half-turn half a full turn

heavier weighs more

hexagon a 2-D shape with six sides

hour a unit of time (60 minutes)

I

hour

irregular not usual/normal

K

kilogram a measurement of weight (1000 grams)

L

least the smallest amount

left a direction; the opposite to right

length how far from one point to another

less not as many

lighter less heavy

line of symmetry a line which divides something into two identical halves

line of symmetry

litre a unit of measurement

longest the largest length

lots of many

M

mass how much an item weighs

measuring cylinder a container to measure liquids

metre a unit of length

millilitre there are 1000 millilitres in one litre

minute there are 60 minutes in one hour

minutes

month there are 12 months in a year: January, February, March, April, May, June, July, August, September, October, November, December

more greater in number or size

most the greatest or largest in number or size

multiple a number that can be divided equally

multiplication a way of calculating the produce of two numbers, shown by the symbol ×

multiply to increase in number

N

notes paper money

number facts calculations to learn by heart

number line a line with points which represent numbers

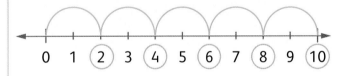

0 1 ② 3 ④ 5 ⑥ 7 ⑧ 9 ⑩

O

octagon a 2-D shape with 8 sides

odd all numbers ending in 1, 3, 5, 7 or 9

ones numbers up to 9

Tens	Ones

order an arrangement of objects

oval shaped like an egg

P

partition separate a number into different parts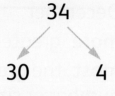

pay give money in return for goods

pentagon a 2-D shape with five sides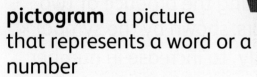

pictogram a picture that represents a word or a number

popular well liked

position place

prism a solid with two identical end faces and three or more rectangular side faces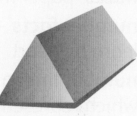

pyramid a solid with triangular sides

Q

quarter(s) something divided by 4

quarter-turn right-angle turn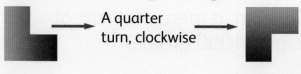

A quarter turn, clockwise

R

rectangle a 2-D shape with two pairs of equal sides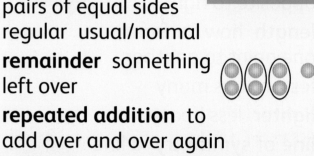

regular usual/normal

remainder something left over

repeated addition to add over and over again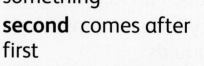

2 + 2 + 2

right a direction; the opposite to left

rotate to turn on a certain point

S

scales used to find the weight of something

second comes after first

semi-circle half of a circle

share to divide something between others

shortest the smallest length or height

shortest

side a line of a shape ← side

sphere a solid round object, like a ball

square a 2-D shape with four sides of equal length

subtract to take away something from another

subtraction a way of finding the difference between two numbers or things

symbol something that represents/stands for something else

symmetrical each half is exactly the same

line of symmetry

T

tallest the largest height

tallest

tally a way of keeping a score or amount

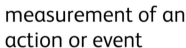

tens shows the tens place value

time a measurement of an action or event

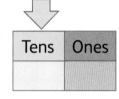

Tens	Ones

times to multiply by another number, shown by the symbol ×

times table a table showing numbers multiplied together

total the answer to an addition calculation

triangle a 2-D shape with three sides

turn to rotate or change position

twice two times

two-digit number a number with a tens digit and a ones digit

V

Venn diagram a diagram with circles to show sets

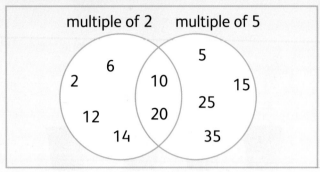

W

week there are 7 days in a week: Monday, Tuesday, Wednesday, Thursday, Friday, Saturday, Sunday

weight how much something weighs

whole-turn a full rotation

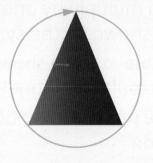

Y

year 365 (or 366) days make a year

CALENDAR

JANUARY

M	T	W	T	F	S	S
				1	2	3
4	5	6	7	8	9	10
11	12	13	14	15	16	17
18	19	20	21	22	23	24
25	26	27	28	29	30	31

FEBRUARY

M	T	W	T	F	S	S
1	2	3	4	5	6	7
8	9	10	11	12	13	14
15	16	17	18	19	20	21
22	23	24	25	26	27	28
29						

MARCH

M	T	W	T	F	S	S
1	2	3	4	5	6	
7	8	9	10	11	12	13
14	15	16	17	18	19	20
21	22	23	24	25	26	27
28	29	30	31			

APRIL

M	T	W	T	F	S	S
				1	2	3
4	5	6	7	8	9	10
11	12	13	14	15	16	17
18	19	20	21	22	23	24
25	26	27	28	29	30	

MAY

M	T	W	T	F	S	S
						1
2	3	4	5	6	7	8
9	10	11	12	13	14	15
16	17	18	19	20	21	22
23 30	24 31	25	26	27	28	29

JUNE

M	T	W	T	F	S	S
		1	2	3	4	5
6	7	8	9	10	11	12
13	14	15	16	17	18	19
20	21	22	23	24	25	26
27	28	29	30			

JULY

M	T	W	T	F	S	S
				1	2	3
4	5	6	7	8	9	10
11	12	13	14	15	16	17
18	19	20	21	22	23	24
25	26	27	28	29	30	31

AUGUST

M	T	W	T	F	S	S
1	2	3	4	5	6	7
8	9	10	11	12	13	14
15	16	17	18	19	20	21
22	23	24	25	26	27	28
29	30	31				

SEPTEMBER

M	T	W	T	F	S	S
			1	2	3	4
5	6	7	8	9	10	11
12	13	14	15	16	17	18
19	20	21	22	23	24	25
26	27	28	29	30		

OCTOBER

M	T	W	T	F	S	S
					1	2
3	4	5	6	7	8	9
10	11	12	13	14	15	16
17	18	19	20	21	22	23
24 31	25	26	27	28	29	30

NOVEMBER

M	T	W	T	F	S	S
	1	2	3	4	5	6
7	8	9	10	11	12	13
14	15	16	17	18	19	20
21	22	23	24	25	26	27
28	29	30				

DECEMBER

M	T	W	T	F	S	S
		1	2	3	4	
5	6	7	8	9	10	11
12	13	14	15	16	17	18
19	20	21	22	23	24	25
26	27	28	29	30	31	